Tonnerre mes chiens!

Tonnerre mes chiens!

A glossary of Louisiana French figures of speech

Compiled and annotated
by Amanda LaFleur

RENOUVEAU PUBLISHING
VILLE PLATTE, LOUISIANA

First Edition

For permission, write:
Amanda LaFleur
205 Pickwick Drive
Lafayette, LA 70503

Book design: Courtney Fuller
Cover design and illustration: Diane Baker
Interior illustrations: Troy Leleux
Photography: Jill Duhon

This book was printed and bound by Patterson Printing
in the United States of America.

ISBN 0-9670838-8-5 (hard cover)
ISBN 0-9670838-9-3 (soft cover)
Library of Congress Card Catalog Number 99-61503

Library of Congress Cataloging-in-Publication Data

LaFleur, Amanda Jane, 1957—
Tonnerre mes chiens!: A glossary of Louisiana French
figures of speech/Amanda LaFleur
p. :ill, ; cm.
Bibliography: p.
Includes index.
1. Cajun French Dialect—Glossaries, Vocabularies, etc.
2. French Language—Dialects. I. Title
PC3680.46 L124
447.976

*Ce livre est dédié
à la mémoire de ma grand-mère,
Merzie Billeaudeaux Brown,
qui était faite du nerf et de la babiche*

et

*au futur de mes enfants,
André et Ariana Giambrone.*

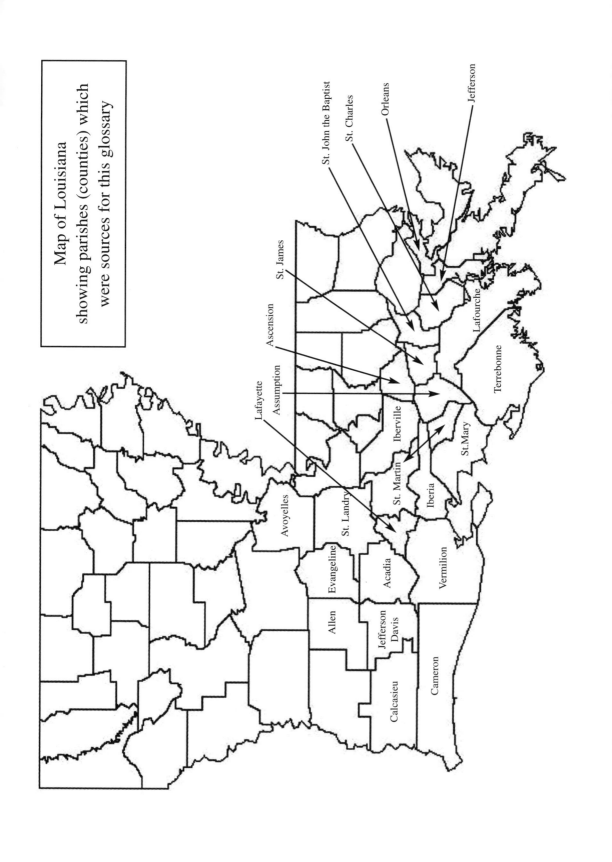

Map of Louisiana
showing parishes (counties) which
were sources for this glossary

Table of Contents

Foreword

Amanda LaFleur's work represents the continuation of an interesting and important vein in Louisiana French studies. During the early 1970s when the Council for the Development of French in Louisiana (CODOFIL) was first reinstating the teaching of French in Louisiana's elementary schools, there was considerable confusion concerning how this would be done. Due to a lack of qualified native Louisiana French teachers, Belgians, French, Québécois, and even a few Tunisians were imported to fill the gap. Understandably, these foreign teachers could not be expected to know enough about the local variety of French to make use of it in their classrooms. It was also CODOFIL policy at the time to focus exclusively on standard scholarly French in the classroom. Some activists felt that this philosophy was pushing the local French dialect back into the same corner where English had kept it in the first half of this century. Some of us argued for Louisianifying the teaching of French in Louisiana. James Donald Faulk, a French teacher in the Crowley area, even devised a method and what he called a textbook designed to help incorporate Cajun French into the classroom. His cause struck an emotional chord in South Louisiana. Parents were concerned that the French their children were learning did not help them communicate easily in their own communities and families. Unfortunately, Faulk's materials were flawed. They were not based on acceptable orthography; Faulk tried to press his pronunciation guide, which was based on English phonetics, into service as a written form. But his basic idea was sound and eventually won over many believers in the educational system.

Over the years, numerous projects have been developed to incorporate Louisiana French language and culture into our classrooms. This excellent study of Cajun and Creole French expressions contributes mightily to that cause. There is a wealth of information included here, all of it meticulously documented. Through this sort of careful and creative exploration of our cultural and linguistic roots, we will eventually be able to claim our rightful territory in the Francophone World. This knowledge will arm not only students of the language but also future poets, songwriters, novelists and playwrights so that the ways that we write, speak and sing the language will be in our own terms and rooted in our own place.

Barry Jean Ancelet
Études Francophones
University of Southwestern Louisiana

Preface

Predictions for the future of the French language in Louisiana were dire when I entered the working world in 1979. As a French teacher, I wanted to participate in the preservation effort, but despite the fact that I had grown up in Cajun country and heard the language all my life, I had only finally become fluent in French after studying it in a foreign country. After my return home, I was eager to add more Louisiana terms to my vocabulary, particularly when I was offered the unique opportunity to teach a class in Cajun French at Comeaux High School in Lafayette in 1984. As part of the class organization, I asked each student to find a mentor in the community, a **"parrain"** or **"marraine"** who spoke the local French and could furnish language and folk traditions corresponding to the themes we would study in class. I knew it would be great for my students to do field work and use their French in authentic ways, but I also figured that it would help me to enrich my own language base.

The first class assignment was relatively straightforward. After studying a few basic salutations, students were asked to collect as many different greeting formulas as possible. I can still remember my great satisfaction when they strode into class a few days later, greeting me with: **Quoi ça dit, madame?"**(literally, *what do you say?*) and **Comment les haricots?**, (literally, *how are the string beans?*). But one response to these formulaic questions was a particular delight:

Mieux que ça et les prêtres seraient jaloux!
Any better than this and the priests would be jealous!

In the days that followed, many students voluntarily chose to use that response when I asked **"Comment ça va?,"** even though they knew shorter and easier ones. I could have taught them those individual words, but by learning words in phrases which reflect our cultural context, they were acquiring something far more lyrical and at the same time useful. A single figure of speech had captured so many elements of Louisiana French culture: humor, Catholicism, an appreciation for hyperbole, and good-natured irreverence for the institutions which we hold dear.

Popular metaphor and figures of speech are the poetry of our everyday communication. They enrich our expression with imbedded meaning, history and a sense of belonging to a particular community. Even when such expressions are used to the point of becoming cliché, they provide us a vehicle for expressing subtleties that individual words or literal expressions lack.

With the advent of French language immersion programs in our schools, the renewed popularity of Cajun music among our young people, and the importance of French to Louisiana's burgeoning tourist industry, we can now realistically believe that French in this area will survive into generations to come. Perhaps in its own way this collection can help revive some figurative expressions for older speakers who may have forgotten them, and at the same time enrich the communication of our new generation of French speakers. A living language does not exist in a vacuum, however. If this work inspires the creation of new metaphors for our time, that will be perhaps the brightest sign of hope for Louisiana French.

Acknowledgements

First, I would like to express my sincere appreciation to the informants, who gave so generously of their time, their knowledge, and their hospitality, in the interest of Louisiana French. This book could not exist without them. Secondly, I want to acknowledge the work of the many Louisiana French scholars whose collections are cited herein. In particular, I want to thank David Lanclos and Allen Simon, present-day observers of figurative language, who have kindly permitted their previously unpublished collections to appear in this glossary.

I am deeply grateful to the National Endowment for the Humanities and the Dewitt Wallace Foundation, which funded the Teacher Scholar Grant for my initial research in 1992, and to the Council on Basic Education and the *Fondation Média-Louisiane*, which granted funding for continued research and final editing respectively.

Many thanks to the University of Southwestern Louisiana for access to its special collections and use of office space. I would particularly like to thank the staff of the Louisiana Room and Barry Ancelet of the Archives of the Center for Acadian and Creole Folklore and Oral History for their generous assistance. Special thanks to Shirley Abshire for teaching me where to look for the stories behind the words.

Thanks to the Hill Memorial Library of Louisiana State University, for access to its collection.

Special thanks to:
• Audrey George, Laïse Ledet, Glen Pitre and David Marcantel, for their help in contacting informants. *Un grand merci* to Audrey for overnight hospitality in her bed and breakfast.
• Greg Wirth, for the Louisiana map;
• Ben Sandmel, for his authorly counsel;
• Phoebe Trotter and Cindy Brown, for taking to the roads with me;
• Becky Brown, Delia Trahan Beaugh, François Gentil, Tom Klingler, Richard Guidry, Danny Povinelli, Laurie Trumps, Seth Johnson and Sandy LaBry, for their careful reading, editing and commentaries at various stages in the development of the manuscript;
• Bill Fontenot, Susan Mopper and Jim Whelan, for their clear and concise explanations of nature's wonders;

• Leo Trahan, Nancy Marks and Colby Marks, for their helpful clarifications in the fields of animal husbandry and horsemanship;

• Eric LaFleur, for his legal and marketing assistance;

• Tony Maida and Shamus Fuller, for their timely rescues in my times of computer crisis;

• Flo LaFleur, for her regular reports on the expressions used in her *bourrée* group, and Dwight LaFleur, for convincing the men at the horse barn to share what they knew (and both of them, for their love and support over forty-two years);

• Troy Leleux and Diane Baker, for their creativity and aesthetic sensibilities;

• Courtney Fuller, for her design, perseverance, professionalism and her relentless good humor;

• Brenda Mounier, for having scouted expressions and left them on my answering machine for seven years, and for being an unfailing source of moral support in all other aspects of this project;

• My wonderful husband, Steve Giambrone, for his sustaining love, encouraging words, thoughtful commentaries, and his unwavering belief in this project and in me.

Introduction

The French language of Louisiana, like the people who speak it, is the product of the vast and varied influences which make this state a cultural treasure trove today. From the early French colonial period to that of Spanish rule, from the first contact with Native Americans through the arrival of African slaves, Acadians, and Caribbean refugees, the French language in Louisiana has adapted to the cultural and natural realities of its home. Louisiana has long been a micro-melting pot. Besides the arrival of Germans, Italians, Koreans, Anglo-Americans and numerous other ethnic groups, new infusions of French-speaking immigrants from various parts of the world have occurred throughout the history of the state. The contact was not just one-way: wealthier families through the turn of the century often sent their children to France for higher education. WWII-era Cajuns served as French interpreters in Europe. And more recently, young CODOFIL scholars have temporarily "exiled" themselves in France, Belgium and Canada in order to master the language of their ancestors.

To speak of Louisiana French simply as an archaic form of the language is to ignore the complexity of influences contributing to its evolution. One has only to visit our Acadian cousins in the Canadian maritimes to recognize that the Louisiana and Canadian-Acadian varieties of French have been independently influenced and changed in ways which make them distinct from each other today, despite similarities dating back to their shared origins. Languages evolve and adapt, or else they die. What is fascinating about Louisiana French is that, despite a general lack of written tradition and a relative isolation from the rest of the French-speaking world for many years, the language has preserved or adapted so many of the metaphors and verbal images of its roots.

Louisiana French possesses a wealth of figurative language. Included in this collection are expressions of many different types, but all have two common characteristics: (1) they evoke imagery that enhances the idea trying to be conveyed and (2) they are formulaic in structure. What we discover in exploring popular Louisiana figures of speech is that many of them which seem so typically local in color can be found, sometimes word for word, in centuries-old texts in France. Some expressions have survived in Louisiana intact into the 20th century, with no shift in structure or meaning. Large numbers of them can still be found in France, too, or in other French-speaking countries, despite the relative isolation of these lands from Louisiana. **Fils de putain *(son of a bitch),*** for example, has been used to insult people since the 11th century. Other expressions have survived but undergone an evolution in meaning. To have **la fale basse *(the craw low)*** in Louisiana is to be hungry. The exact same expression means "to be tired or depressed" in Canada and "to have a hard time making a living" in western France (whose Norman dialect gave us the word **fale** in the first place).

Other figures of speech have evolved in structure or word choice, though their meaning remains intact. While the simile **mentir comme un arracheur de dents** *(to lie like a tooth puller)* is now considered outdated in France, particularly with the advent of anesthesia and other medical palliatives, Louisiana French has maintained the comparison and even added a modern variant: **mentir comme un dentiste (to lie like a dentist).** However one looks at these phenomena, it is impressive that certain images or motifs remain attached to a language even as its other attributes evolve and transform with time.

Does this mean that none of Louisiana French is native to the state? Absolutely not. However, even expressions that are unique to Louisiana often embody structures and styles that link them to the rest of the francophone world. When a Cajun talks about making **gombo de babine** *(pout gumbo)* after a failed political campaign, he is tapping into the same linguistic heritage which prompts his European cousin to talk about having to eat his wife's **soupe à la grimace** *(grimace soup)* when he gets home late for dinner. Our shared subconscious "feel" for the French language makes it more natural to put words together in one way than another, so that certain rhythms and structures recur. **Un défonceur de portes ouvertes (a breaker down of open doors)** in Louisiana is a braggart, "a bag of wind." Similarly, **un avaleur de citadelles (a swallower of citadels)** in France is an "armchair quarterback," one who bores others with treatises on how things would be better if he were in charge [Edouard 1967].

What can we gain from the study of Louisiana French figures of speech? Perhaps we can hope to better understand how varieties of the same language evolve and remain the same over time. Imagine for a moment the case of identical twins separated at birth. Though their genetic makeups are indistinguishable, each lives through different experiences, environmental influences and personal choices which contribute to the development of two distinct, albeit similar individuals. In trying to define Louisiana French, it is important to keep in mind that the complete picture is not only in the "genetic code" of vocabulary and grammatical structure, but also in the poetry of the language, the imagery which speakers have chosen to keep, to reject, to adapt and to invent as the language has evolved over time. All of these elements come together to form the personality of Louisiana French as it exists today. I hope that the figurative expressions you find in this collection will also help you to better understand the language and the people to whom they belong.

About the collection

The expressions in this book were taken from a data base of over two thousand five hundred expressions collected over a period of approximately six years. In 1992, with the assistance of a Teacher Scholar Grant from the National Endowment for the Humanities, I was able to begin gathering data for this project. I interviewed over 70 Louisiana French speakers and consulted 30 doctoral and master's theses and other works dealing with regional French dialects of the state. Most of the interviews were conducted in 1992 and 1993, and thus represent contemporary language. The written sources, on the other hand, span a period from 1931 to 1992. In all, these sources represent 23 different Louisiana parishes.

Beginning with a base list of approximately 25 expressions, I interviewed fluent speakers of Louisiana French, asking them if they had heard or used these expressions and what they understood them to mean. Informants were also encouraged to comment on the nature of the expression (Is it used more commonly in certain contexts? Is it vulgar? Is it used ironically? Is it heard frequently or rarely today?) The expressions, designed to "prime the pump," gave examples of what I was looking for and helped informants to recall variants or other expressions with similar themes or structures. Each new interview yielded dozens more expressions to add to the master list.

With written sources, which consisted mainly of regional glossaries, I noted expressions which were metaphorical, added those to the master list, and tried to verify them along with others I had collected. Unfortunately, some collections only listed figures of speech without indicating the metaphorical meanings of the expressions, or gave other figures of speech, now out of use, as definitions. There are many of these whose meanings I have still not been able to ascertain. Other expressions appear to have fallen out of common usage, since I was unable to find contemporary informants who were familiar with them. Many of these are included in the glossary.

During the summer of 1995, with the assistance of a grant from the Council on Basic Education, I researched the etymologies and histories of some of the expressions in the collection, using reference works housed in the library of the University of Southwestern Louisiana. That work produced many of the annotations you will read.

Generally, I chose to include in this glossary expressions whose existence was verified by at least two informants. This does not necessarily indicate that a given expression would be known throughout French-speaking Louisiana. If several variant meanings were given, I included them. If a variant appeared to be regional, I indicated as much. If the expression came from another collection, such as one of the dissertations or theses previously mentioned, I assumed that the collector had some evidence that the expression was in common use in his region, even if no mention was made of methodology in the work itself. When the expression cited from another collection has not been verified by contemporary sources, the author and year of publication of the work are indicated with the entry. In the same way, interesting expressions reported by one informant but not verified by others indicate the informant's code with the entry.

This collection is a representative sampling of expressions which are part of the Cajun repertoire, but also includes some Creole expressions, as well as some of what used to be called "colonial French," the variety which was spoken by educated classes who had more regular contact with New Orleans and Europe. Today, linguists generally seem to concur that the French spoken in Louisiana no longer fits the "three type" paradigm but is better characterized as a continuum along which different speakers can be placed or even move.

Figures of speech in this book were chosen because they were the most interesting or had interesting histories. I do not pretend to have systematically pinpointed the regions where individual expressions are used, nor did I systematically leave out all expressions which seem to have disappeared in recent years. Finally, this collection is far from exhaustive. I would be delighted to hear from readers who would like to share expressions from their communities, as well as those who have comments and variants to add to those already in the glossary. Please send correspondence regarding this collection to TMC, c/o Renouveau Publishing, 205 Pickwick Drive, Lafayette, LA 70503, or by email to tmchiens@aol.com. You can help make the second edition even bigger and better!

How to Read an Entry

If you are a Louisianian who speaks French but doesn't read it, try looking at the literal English translation first (i.e., the words in parentheses after the main entry). Then, when you look at the main entry, use the English translation to help you read the French. If you're a Cajun or Creole, most of the words will be familiar to you.

If you read French but are unfamiliar with the Louisiana variety of the language, use the literal translation to help you with terms unfamiliar to you. Though I occasionally note a few general phonetic features in the annotations, I did not attempt to render the pronunciation of each expression phonetically. The large number of regional variants in pronunciation among Louisiana French speakers would make such notation too cumbersome to read.

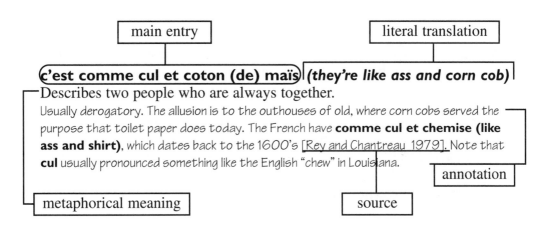

Main entry: This is the featured expression. Verb forms are usually given as infinitives, except when a sample sentence seems to better illustrate the expression. If parts of the expression are optional or variable, they are enclosed in brackets (ex. **déchirer la couverte [en deux]**). Additional words which help to situate the grammatical context in which an expression is used appear in curly brackets **(ex. faire manger du chien enragé {à quelqu'un})**. The slash mark is used in cases where it is not clear which of two homophones is intended in meaning (ex. **l'amour n'a pas de faim/fin** could mean "love has no hunger" or "love has no end").

Literal translation: This is the word-for-word English translation of the expression. In general, I have tried to give translations from Louisiana French, but the reader should keep in mind that, in some cases, the metaphorical meaning is the only vestige of the expression left in Louisiana. In those cases, the reader will see the notation IF, which indicates that the literal meaning given is from international French and would not necessarily be recognized in Louisiana. Occasionally, when the translation from IF is explained in the annotation, or when the word itself is a new form, the literal translation is omitted.

Metaphorical meaning: This is the message "beyond the words" that the expression carries. I've tried to avoid using English figures of speech and slang as main definitions because these can change or be lost in the course of time, but sometimes equivalent English figures of speech are given in quotes (ex. to behave arrogantly and self-righteously; to "get on one's high horse").

Annotation: This is information which can help the reader to learn about the origins of the expression, contexts in which it is likely to be used, and similar expressions used in other French-speaking countries. It may also include descriptions of some special features of the Louisiana French language or local culture. The font for annotations is different from that of the metaphorical meaning.

Source: If an expression has been verified by at least two informants, then it is considered to be in common usage and no source is cited. However, three types of sources can be found within certain entries:

(1) *Authors of collections of Louisiana expressions.* In cases where an expression from one of these collections was not verified by any contemporary informants, the source is listed by author and year of publication (ex. [Calais 1968]). Further information on these works is listed in the **Bibliography of Louisiana Collections**.

(2) *Informants.* In cases where an informant is the sole source of an expression included in this glossary, a letter code representing the informant is included in brackets (ex. [PNA]). Note that this does not mean that the expression is unknown by other speakers, but simply that it was not verified by any of the sources interviewed or quoted. Names and home parishes of informants are listed in the **Informants** section at the back of the book.

(3) *Secondary sources.* This will give the authors of secondary sources used to obtain information about origins and usage of expressions (ex. [Rey and Chantreau 1979]). They are listed in the **Bibliography of Other Sources** at the back of the book.

Abbreviations Used in this Glossary

- adj.   Adjective

- adv.   Adverb

- f.   Feminine

- i.   Intransitive

- IF   International French *(expressions which would be understood in most French-speaking countries)*

- LF   Louisiana French

- m.   Masculine

- n.   Noun

- pl.   Plural

- s.   Singular

- t.   Transitive

- v.   Verb

Va-t-et-vient

Comings and Goings

Knowing how to greet people and take leave within a community is essential to one's ability to identify as an insider. Even business people in South Louisiana who speak little or no French often learn some of these salutations because they know it's a key to setting the tone for successfully "connecting" with their clients.

Here are some interesting alternatives to **comment ça va?** *when asking how things are going:*

comment ça se brasse? *(how are things stirring up?)*
How are you? How are things?

A cordial response would be **ça se brasse**! This greeting is very common.

comment ça ballote? *(how are things balancing?)*
How are you? How are things?

comment ça boulotte? *(how are things working/turning?)*
How are you? How are things?

This expression is well-known in France.

comment ça se plume? *(how is it plucking?)*
How are you? How are things?

A positive cordial response would be **ça se plume!** The verb **plumer** means to pluck feathers. A metaphor which compares life to plucking fowl (a task which is at times easier than at others) would certainly be well-grounded in traditional rural Louisiana. My friend RJG relates that one of his aunts sometimes responded **"Il y a des repoussants, mais ça se plume!"** (**"There are pin feathers, but it's plucking!"**).

comment c'est? *(how is it?)*
How are you? How are things?

comment le cabri apporte sa queue? *(how is the goat carrying his tail?)*
How are you? How are things?

This Avoyelles Parish expression [Jeansonne 1938] doesn't appear to be common today, but it deserves to be revived. The word **cabri,** which refers to a baby goat in modern IF, is used in the generic sense of "goat" in both Louisiana and French-speaking Caribbean islands such as Guadeloupe.

comment les cannes sont? *(how is the sugar cane?)*
How are you? How are things?

This humorous Bayou Lafourche greeting, contributed by the KJ family, is based on the play between the words **cannes sont** and **caneçons,** a common alternate pronunciation of **caleçons (underpants)**. While ostensibly asking someone how his cane crop is doing, the speaker is also jokingly asking about the condition of his underwear.

comment les haricots? *(how are the green beans?)*
How are you? How are things?

Note that in Louisiana one typically pronounces a liaison in **les-z-haricots**.

When things are going very well, we might respond using one of these:

ça va sur des roulettes *(it's going on little wheels)*
It's going very well.
Also documented in France as early as 1826 [Duneton 1990].

mieux que ça et les prêtres seraient jaloux *(any better than this, and the priests would be jealous)*
Things are going very well.
Since many Catholics still view the parish priest as one whose life is free of the real world concerns of laymen, anyone whose situation could "make a priest jealous" is in a very enviable position. French Louisianians' fervent Catholicism has rarely hindered them from poking fun at the clergy, and francophones elsewhere in the world are equally disposed. In Acadian Canada, one can be **hypocrite comme un prêtre à talons hauts** *(as hypocritical as a priest in high heeled shoes)*. In 17th century France, a **fils de prêtre** *(son of a priest)* was one who repeated himself in speaking, and a proverb of the same period advises **qui veut tenir nette maison, il n'y faut prêtre ni pigeon** *(he who wants to keep a clean house should let neither priests nor pigeons enter within)* [Duneton 1990].

mieux que ça serait une bêtise *(any better than this would be a joke, ridiculous)*
Things are going very well.
Variant: **mieux que ça serait des bêtises**.

mieux que ça serait de la gourmandise *(any better than this would be gluttony)*
Things are going very well.

mieux que ça serait un enterrement *(any better than this would be a funeral /burial)*
Things are going very well.
This one can also be used ironically to mean "things couldn't be worse."

mieux que ça serait un cas d'hôpital *(any better than this would be a hospital case)*.
Things are going very well.
This one can also be used ironically to mean "things couldn't be worse."

Life, of course, is not always a bed of roses.

train des vieux *(at the rhythm of old people)*
O.K. for my age; slowly and carefully.

The implication is "I've got the usual aches and pains and I don't get around so easily anymore, but I won't bore you with all that." When a friend's father in Breaux Bridge started up a Cajun band with several other local octagenarians, they named their lively group **Train des Vieux**, playing on two meanings of **train** (*rhythm* and *noise*) in LF.

ça gain pou couri (*it has to "go"*)
Things are O.K. I'm making it.

This Creole idiom, along with its Cajun equivalent **il faut que "ça va,"** expresses an acceptance of the situation as it is, along the lines of "it wouldn't do any good to complain."

Here are a few greetings used for specialized situations:

le docteur après la mort! (*the doctor after the death!*)
Too late [Faulk 1977]!

This might be said, for example, when someone arrives just after an event has taken place.

quoi ça dit? (*what do you say?*)
What's up? What's new? What's happening?

The usual response is **pas grand-chose (*not much*)**.

en parlant des anges, on voit leurs ailes (*in speaking of angels, one sees their wings*)

This expression is used to mark the arrival of someone who's just recently been the topic of conversation. Depending on the person in question, one might alternatively use the counterpart **en parlant du diable, on voit sa queue (*in speaking of the devil, one sees his tail*)**. The French use **quand on parle du loup on voit sa queue (*when you talk about the wolf, you see its tail*)**.

quand on parle de la bête, on voit sa tête (*when you talk about the beast, you see its head*)
See **en parlant des anges, on voit leurs ailes**.

est-ce que t'amènes la pluie? (*are you bringing the rain with you?*)
This is used to greet a visitor you haven't seen in a long time.

t'as venu pour une braise? (*did you come for a hot coal?*)
This greeting, furnished by LLE in Terrebonne Parish, is used to welcome visitors who haven't come by in a long time. The insinuation, it appears, is that the person has only come now that he has a pressing need. Note that in LF, the past tense of the verb **venir** is in most cases conjugated with **avoir**.

Variant: **t'as venu pour du feu? (*did you come for fire?*)**

After the conversation is over, leaving has its own rituals:

c'est l'heure qu'on lève la paille *(it's time to raise the straw)*
It's time to go.
The **paille** in this context is a straw hat.

c'est l'heure qu'on lève la patte *(it's time to raise a foot)*
It's time to go.
The oral similarity between **patte** and **paille** in this expression and the expression just above it suggests that one of these might have developed as a variant of the other.

c'est l'heure qu'on casse le rond *(it's time to break the circle)*
It's time to break up the party or conversation (and go home).
In political conversation, it can also refer to breaking up a faction or machine.
Variant: **c'est l'heure qu'on casse le cercle.**

on a plein d'huile dans la lampe *(we still have plenty of oil in the lamp)*
You don't have to go yet; it's still early.
As in English, this is as often a stock phrase for "goodbye" as it is a sincere invitation to stay.

on va se revoir [plus tard]! *(we'll see each other [later]!)*
This form is at least as common as **au revoir,** if not moreso. One also hears simply the elliptical version **plus tard!**

revenez! *(Come back!)*
This is the typical way a merchant would say good-bye to customers, and is certainly influenced by the Southern standard "Y'all come back now!" The forms **reviens!** and **reviens back!** are also common.

t'à l'heure! *(in a minute!)*
See you soon!
From **à tout à l'heure!**

Les amis et les amours

Friends and Lovers

*Friends and lovers provide ample fodder for those who enjoy creatively describing
human relationships. Romance naturally inspires sentiment, whether it be empathy,
jealousy or disdain, and its ups and downs are as old as the Garden of Eden.
Friendship, too, is a universal theme.*

Chapitre 2

Togetherness and lack thereof:

ça porte les mêmes caleçons *(they wear the same underpants)*
They are always together.

casser la paille *(to break the straw)*
To sever relations.
Though it often refers to couples who break up, this expression can refer to friends or business relationships, too. According to *Le Trésor de la Langue Française*, the France French version **rompre la paille** has its origins in customs of the 12th century. In that predominantly illiterate feudal society, contracts were made by oral ceremony in front of a number of witnesses. The presentation of a straw of grain symbolized an oath of allegiance, and conversely, the breaking of a straw marked the severing of relations.

casser sa vaisselle *(to break one's dishes)*
(1) To break up (of a couple or household).
(2) To fall down and hurt oneself.

ça chie dans le même sac *(they shit in the same sack)*
They are two of a kind, equally bad [MBG].

c'est comme chat et chien *(they're like cat and dog)*
To not get along well; to quarrel habitually.
Variants: **s'adonner comme chat et chien *(to get along like cat and dog)***
          s'adonner comme chien et chat *(to get along like dog and cat)*

c'est comme cul et coton [de] maïs *(they're like ass and corn cob)*
Describes two people who are always together.
Usually derogatory. The allusion is to the outhouses of old, where corn cobs served the purpose that toilet paper does today. In France, the structurally similar **comme cul et chemise *(like ass and shirt)***, which dates back to the 1600s, is used to convey the same figurative meaning [Duneton 1990].

c'est comme le feu et l'eau *(they're like fire and water)*
They're always quarreling.

c'est comme Saint Roch et son chien *(they're like St. Roc and his dog)*
These two people are always together.
St. Roch (Rocco) was a 13th century Italian saint who, afflicted by the plague, was nursed back to health by his faithful dog. The expression was popular in 18th century France [Rey and Chantreau 1979].

c'est la faim et la soif *(it's hunger and thirst)*
(1) One is as bad as the other [Saucier 1956].
(2) Humorous reference to two poor people who have gotten married [Calais 1968].
A variant on the same motif, **la faim a rencontré la soif** *(hunger has met thirst),* is said when two unattractive people have gotten married.

c'est le bras droit de... *(it's the right arm of...)*
Refers to a very dependable friend of someone.

c'est un "cher" ici, "cher" là-bas *(it's "darling" here and "darling" there)*
Refers to a couple who make a show of affection in public, but who fight frequently in private [Simon 1991].
Cher is French Louisiana's favorite term of endearment.

Chiquette et Berlingue
"A ridiculous or absurd-looking couple" [Voohries 1949].

comme des patates et des puces *(like potatoes and fleas)*
Refers to people or things which go together naturally [Lanclos 1992].

déchirer la couverte [en deux] *(to tear the blanket [in two])*
To separate, of a couple.
This reference to marital breakups has several popular variants: **déchirer la couverture en deux** [Hickman 1940] and **déchirer la couilte**, both of which describe some type of coverlet for the conjugal bed. Given that community-made quilts were traditional and valued wedding gifts, the symbol becomes all the more poignant. By extension, some speakers use these expressions to refer to the break up of any relationship.

donner son capot {à quelqu'un} *(to give {someone} his jacket/coat)*
To reject or break up with a suitor [Hickman 1940].

être à dos *(to be back to back)*
To be on bad terms in a relationship.

être en bisbille {avec quelqu'un}
To be on bad terms with someone [Calais 1968].
This expression also has been used in France [Deak and Deak 1959].

être en divorce *(to be divorced)*
To be at odds with someone, though not necessarily of a couple.

faire barouche
To break up, to have a disagreement.
I have only heard this expression in the Terrebonne/Lafourche area.
Variant: **avoir barouche.**

Matrimony and such:

accolé *(stuck)*
Of a couple, living together without being married [Guilbeau 1950].

s'accoupler *(to couple)*
(1) Of a couple, to live together without being legally married.
(2) For Catholics, to live together without being married in the Catholic Church [Guilbeau 1950].

s'adopter *(to adopt each other)*
Of a couple, to live together without being married.
Euphemistic.

s'amancher *(to hook up)*
(1) Of a couple, to live together without being married.
(2) To be politically united with someone.

se casser le cou *(to break one's neck)*
To get married [Parr 1940, Brandon 1955].

elle porte les culottes *(she wears the pants)*
She is the dominant person of the couple or household.
This is a good example of a metaphorical image which has found a place in practically every European language. According to Duneton 1990, the concept predates the fashion, as it was **haut-de-chaussés *(breeches)*** that domineering women wore in the 17th century version of this expression.

faire chaudière ensemble *(to make a cooking pot together)*
To get married [Hickman 1940].
Chaudière, which typically describes the heavy, cast iron pot used commonly for cooking in Louisiana, has come to be the generic translation for **pot**. It is, of course, a classic symbol of domestic life.

jouqués *(yoked together)*
Of a couple, living together without being married.
The same metaphorical image is evoked in **se macorner.**

se macorner *(to be yoked together)*
Of a couple, to live together without being married.
The verb is from the Spanish **mancornar**, to yoke animals together. Calais 1968 also gives the meaning "to get dressed up," for **se macorner**, but I was unable to verify that usage in recent years. The noun form **macornage** (m.) also exists to describe amourous cohabitation. See also **s'amancher**.
Variants: **s'amacorner**
       se mancorner.

mets pas ton doigt entre l'arbre et l'écorce *(don't put your finger between the tree and the bark)*
Don't get mixed up in other people's marital problems [Simon 1991].
Proverbial.

la mort n'a pas de faim/fin *(death has no hunger/end)*
Proverb cited when two elderly people marry.

se placer *(to place oneself)*
To live in an unmarried state with a person of the opposite sex.
The past participle **placé** *(placed)* is also mentioned in Calais 1968 as meaning "in a state of concubinage."

prends mari, prends pays *(take the husband, take the country)*
When a woman marries, she must accommodate herself to her husband's habits, family, etc.
This proverbial expression was traditionally used to remind wives to subjugate their own wishes to those of their spouses.

sauter le manche à balai *(to jump the broomstick)*
To live together without being married.
The abbreviated locution **sauter le balai** *(to jump the broom)* is also well-known. Tradition has it that in isolated areas of Louisiana where priests were not in residence, as well as in black slave communities, a couple wanting to live together as married could ceremonially jump a broomstick. This act sanctioned their union within the community until the next visit by clergy who sanctified it. By extension, a couple who has "jumped the broom" metaphorically is living together "without benefit of clergy."

Les batailles et les chicanes

Fights and Arguments

From bar room brawls to domestic squabbles to children's quarrels, folks have always tended to describe their personal conflicts with colorful language.

Chapitre 3

abominer (v.t.) *(to abhor)*
(1) To beat; to whip [Dugas 1935].
(2) To scold; to say unpleasant things to.
(3) To annoy; to bother [Trahan 1936].

agoniser (v.t) *(to agonise)*
(1) To insult; to bawl out.
(2) To vex beyond endurance; to aggravate.
(3) To overwhelm [Olivier 1937].

amener au bercail *(to bring to the fold)*
To make one obey, to make one give in [Jeansonne 1938].
In IF, the metaphor **ramener au bercail** *(to bring back to the fold)* is used in describing a religious renewal.

assaper (v.t.)
To beat or to whip [Olivier 1937].

assommer (v.t.) *(to beat up)*
(1) To beat up or overcome someone in a fight.
(2) To get the best of someone.

avoir castile avec {quelqu'un}
To quarrel with someone [Saucier 1956].

avoir des mots avec {quelqu'un} *(to have words with {someone})*
To have a quarrel with someone [Calais 1968].
Variant: **avoir des paroles avec {quelqu'un}** *(to have words with {someone})* [PNA].

babiller (v.t.) *(to babble IF)*
To scold; to reprimand or chide [Trahan 1936].

bâcler (v.t.)
To overcome; to beat up [Daigle 1934].

le Bon Dieu descend pas pour bûcher *(God does not come down to destroy)*
Justice is not always immediate, but it will prevail in the end [Simon 1991].
Proverbial.

boucher (v.t.) *(to plug; to stop up)*
To silence; to get the better of someone in an argument [Olivier 1937].

bouche-trou (n.f.) *(hole-plug)*
"A ready response;" a quick retort [Hurst 1938].

bourlinguer (v.t.) *(to roam the seas, to travel a lot IF)*
To maltreat [Babin 1937].

brûlée (n.f.) *(a burning)*
Whipping; thrashing [Viator 1935].

bûcher (v.t.) *(to chop [a piece of wood])*
To whip considerably [Jeansonne 1938].

chauffer (v.t.) *(to heat)*
To scold; to reprimand or chide [Granier 1939].

chien mord chien *(dog bites dog)*
"It takes one to know one;" "birds of a feather flock together"
[Simon 1991].

crache dans l'air, ça tombe sur le [bout du] nez *(spit in the air, it falls on [the tip of] your nose)*
If you speak ill of others, it comes back to haunt you.
This proverb is used as a reprimand to one who criticizes others or is sanctimonious.

donner un cataplasme {à quelqu'un} *(to give a poultice {to someone})*
To scold someone profusely; to tell someone off.
Variant: **passer un cataplâme à quelqu'un** [PF].

être derrière {quelqu'un} *(to be behind {someone})*
"To torment or nag someone" [Jeansonne 1938].

faire chiquer poteaux {à quelqu'un} *(to make {someone}... chew posts)*
To best someone in competition [Hickman 1940].

faire manger de l'avoine {à quelqu'un} *(to make {someone} eat oats)*
To best someone in competition [Hickman 1940].

faire "poteau, Caillette" {à quelqu'un} *(to do "post, Caillette" {to someone})*
To make obey; to force to give in [Jeansonne 1938].
The command **"Poteau, Caillette!"** was commonly given to milk cows to tell them to get into position for milking.

foutre une chauffe {à quelqu'un} *(to throw a "heat" {at someone})*
"To bawl someone out" [Grenier 1939].

lire un catéchisme {à quelqu'un} *(to read a catechism {to someone})*
To tell someone off [Lanclos 1992].

massacrer la couenne {à quelqu'un} *(to massacre {someone's} hide)*
To give someone a beating [Parr 1940].
Couenne refers specifically to pig skin which has been scraped in the butchering process. It is often deep-fried to make **gratons** *(cracklings).*

mettre un apostrophe {à quelqu'un} *(to put an apostrophe {to someone})*
To slap someone [Dugas 1935].
In IF, the term **apostrophe** refers to the rhetorical device known as "apostrophe," as well as the punctuation marks which usually set it off. By extension, in IF the word has come to mean a "strong remark or verbal injury addressed directly to a person." Indeed Trahan 1936 gives this as one meaning for the verbal form **apostrophier (v.t.)** *(to address insultingly),* in addition to the meaning "to slap."

passer {quelqu'un} à la bastringue *(to pass {someone} through the triangle)*
To beat up someone [Lanclos 1992].
In LF, **la bastringue,** also referred to as a **ti-fer** *(little iron),* is a traditional rhythm instrument in Cajun music. During a lively two-step, it is beaten with great enthusiasm. In IF, it is a masculine noun which describes a public hall dance and by extension, noise.

passer {quelqu'un} à la baleine *(to pass {someone} under the whalebone)*
To whip someone [Phillips 1936].
Whalebone, or "baleen" as it was sometimes referred to in English, is actually not the bone but the flexible, seive-like cartilage which certain species of whales used to filter water, allowing minute food particles to enter their digestive systems. It was used into the the twentieth century to make corset stays among other things, and the term **baleine** eventually came to refer to "stays" (corset or bonnet, for example) made of any material. The flexible yet stiff quality of stays made them natural for delivering beatings.

piler (v.t.) *(to grind, crush)*
To trample; to beat [Granier 1939].
The noun form **une pile,** "a beating," was also cited [Jeansonne 1938, Granier 1939].

piloter *(to lead, to pilot)*
(1) (v.t.) To trample [Granier 1939].
(2) (v.i.) To step randomly and carelessly.

racler (v.t.) *(to scrape)*
To whip.
The noun form **raclée (n.f.)** has the metaphorical meaning of "whipping" in Louisiana as well as France. Evangeline Parish area speakers also use the variant **une raclure**.

ramasser (v.t.) *(to pick up again)*
To correct someone in a brusque way [ABR].

rancée (n.f)
A whipping [Coco 1933].

rancer (v.t.)
To beat or whip [PNA].

rançure (n.f.)
A whipping [PNA].

roussequette
A spanking or beating [KAG].

roussetée (n.f.)
A series of blows; a severe beating [Phillips 1936].

rousseture (n.f.)
A whipping [Granier 1939].

saboulée (n.f.) *(a shake IF)*
Series of blows [Phillips 1936].

sabouler (v.t.) *(to shake IF)*
To scold [Granier 1939].

sacrer une gratte {à quelqu'un} *(to give a scraping {to someone})*
To beat someone [OV].

salade (n.f.) *(a salad)*
A slap [Guilbeau 1950].

se souffler dans les narines *(to breathe in each other's nostrils)*
(1) To get physically close in a conflict or argument.
(2) To be on the verge of fighting.

tamiser (v.t.) *(to sift)*
(1) To beat up; to give a beating to [MM].
(2) To scrutinize carefully [PNA].

Les soûls et les fous

Drunks and Crazies

There are lots of euphemisms available to describe altered psychological states. Mental illness and alcoholism have tragic and yet often humorous faces, too. Perhaps the most unsettling thing about them is that we are all attracted to the sensation of joyful abandon and yet live in fear of the terrible affliction of being out of control. There but for the grace of God....

Chapitre 4

About drinking:

à jeun *(fasting)*
Not drinking, "on the wagon."

biture (f.)
A drinking spree, as seen in the expressions **faire une biture, foutre une biture,** and **prendre une biture *(to get drunk)*,** documented by Granier 1939, Hurst 1938, Voohries 1949, and Calais 1968.
Parr 1940 also gives the verb form **se biter**. The adjective **bite** (drunk) is quite common, and perhaps because of the alliterative similarity between it and **bêtail**, not to mention the suggestion of "beastly" behavior associated with over imbibing, the term **bitail** (typically pronounced with the short "i" sound as in English) has also come to function as an adjective meaning "extremely drunk," even in Cajun English dialect. Etymologists place the origins of **biture** in the 1500s, where it refers to the length of cable released to let down a ship's anchor. It is derived from **bitte**, the piece of wood around which the ship's cables were wound. **Se donner une bonne biture** meant literally "to pull enough anchor cable," and by metaphorical extension, "to take as much as one can." In the 19th century, the term **biture** evolved to mean metaphorically "a copious meal," and later "a strong dose of spirits" [Duneton 1990, Rey and Chantreau 1979].

boire comme si on n'avait pas de fond *(drink as if one were bottomless)*
To drink excessively [Brandon 1955].

boire comme un chien *(to drink like a dog)*
To drink excessively [Brandon 1955].

boire comme un poisson *(to drink like a fish)*
To drink excessively.

boire comme un tablier *(to drink like an apron)*
To drink excessively [Saucier 1956].
Evidently, **tablier** is derived from **Templier**, a member of the secret order of Knights Templar. Duneton 1990 documents **boire comme un Templier** as early as mid-16th century France.

boire comme un trou *(to drink like a hole)*
To drink excessively.
This expression dates back to at least 17th century France [Duneton 1990].

un buveur de lait *(a milk drinker)*
One who does not drink alcohol, a "teetotaler."

caler (v.i.) *(to sink)*
To drink alcohol [Bernard 1933].

il crache pas dans la bouteille *(he doesn't spit in the bottle)*
He is a heavy drinker.

dans les brindezingues
Completely drunk [Pirkle 1935].
According to Duneton 1990, this expression has its origins in the archaic term **brinde**, meaning a toast, which was commonly used in 17th century France.

dans son vinaigre *(in one's vinegar)*
Drunk [Phillips 1936].

deux doigts d'une baille à pied de... *(two fingers in a foot tub of...)*
A large drink (ironic).
This humorous reference plays on the contrast between "two fingers," a usual measure of liquor in a glass, and the amount of the same it would take to fill a wide tub to the same measure. The variant **deux doigts d'une baille** *(two fingers of a washtub)* conjures up an even more exaggerated image, since a washtub is bigger than a foottub.

en boisson *(in drink)*
Drunk [Calais 1968].
This expression is also known in Quebec [Robinson and Smith 1984].

flanquer une pointe *(to fling a point)*
To get drunk [Coco 1933].

se foutre une cuite *(to give oneself a cooking)*
To get drunk [Voohries 1949 and Calais 1968].
One could also say **prendre une cuite** [Pirkle 1935]. This expression is documented in 19th century France, though the metaphorical connection between being "cooked" and being "drunk" goes back much farther. The term **cuit** was used figuratively to mean "drunk" as early as 1660 (*Le Nouveau Petit Robert* 11993).

se foutre une guinguette
To get drunk [Calais 1968].
In modern IF, **une guinguette** is a type of tavern.

glacé *(glazed, iced)*
Drunk.

s'insulter les foies *(to insult one's liver)*
To drink too much.
The reference, of course, is to the damage done to one's liver by alcohol.

manier la tapette *(to handle the cork hammer)*
To be a heavy drinker [Viator 1935].
The **tapette** is a flexible hammer or wooden tool used to push corks into bottles.

se péter une ribote *(to throw oneself a celebration)*
To get drunk [PNA].

pinteur *(a pint-drinker)*
A heavy drinker [Hurst 1938].
Une pinte is a drinking cup.

piqué *(stung)*
Drunk [Buchanan 1931].
In LF the verb **piquer** more commonly refers to sexual activity.

prendre une pipine
To get drunk.
Variants: **avoir une pipine**
          se tenir une pipine

ressembler le diable avant jour *(to look like the devil before daylight)*
To look terrible (said of one who has spent the night out carousing) [Lanclos 1992].

rond *(round)*
Drunk.

sac à boisson *(a drink sack)*
A drunkard [Phillips 1936].

saucé *(sauced)*
Drunk.

soiffeur *(an habitually thirsty person)*
A drunkard [Calais 1968].

soûl comme un cochon *(as drunk as a pig)*
Very drunk.

soûl comme une grive *(as drunk as a robin)*
Very drunk.
Robins actually do get drunk and behave erratically after eating fermented berries from bushes and trees. They are not the lone species to imbibe, since the expression **soûl comme un tchoc** *(as drunk as a blackbird)* is also common in LF. In fact, local naturalist Jim Whelan recalls an incident in Metairie in the 1970s when **ciriers** (cedar waxwings) inebriated by fermented berries of pyrocantha bushes planted along Interstate 10 began flying into traffic and posing a hazard to drivers. The trees had to be chemically treated so that they would not produce fruit. The term **grive** in LF refers to the American robin, but in France it describes more generally the thrush family, of which the American robin is a member. **Soûl comme une grive** described drunkards in France as early as the 17th century [Duneton 1990]. (Note that the **rouge-gorge**, a European robin, is not the same species as the American robin.)

soûl en farine *(drunk in flour)*
Very drunk.

tchac (adj.)
Very drunk.
The variant pronunciation **tchoc** possibly developed by association with the expression **soûl comme un tchoc** *(as drunk as a blackbird)*. The verb form **se tchaquer** means "to get drunk."

tchanfré *(camphored)*
Very drunk [Parr 1940].
The spelling here is Parr's, a phonetic rendering of the local pronunciation of **camphré**, which suggests both the potent smell and anesthetic properties of camphor.

tenir une brique *(to hold a brick)*
To be drunk [Hickman 1940].

toqué (adj.)
(1) Very drunk [Granier 1939].
(2) Crazy (Evangeline and Vermilion Parishes).

tricoler (v.i.)
To stagger from intoxication [Babin 1937].

vin à vingt batailles au gallon *(wine which gets 20 fights to the gallon)*
Very strong wine [Voohries 1949].
Though the source of this expression dates to 1949, modern-day concern with gas mileage makes it a particularly humorous and timely play on words.

About mental instability:

avoir une calebasse pour sa tête *(to have a gourd for a head)*
To be foolish [Viator 1935].

baranquer *(to sway, to teeter totter)*
To talk out of one's mind.

battre la berloque *(to beat the "drums")*
To talk deliriously or to ramble in speech; (by extension) to be deranged or delirious.
This expression, which is also still heard in France, has its origins in the military. **La berloque** (also spelled **breloque**) was the drum roll sounded to call soldiers to meals or to break up the ranks. Its irregular and roughshod rhythm is evoked in speech which has the same characteristics. In France, **berloque** can also refer to something which is shoddy or of poor quality, and indeed Guilbeau 1950 gives "said of an old, dilapidated thing" as his commentary on **battre la berloque** as used in Lafourche Parish.

couillon comme la lune *(crazy as the moon)*
Stupid, foolish, crazy.
This simile recalls popular belief about the moon's effects on mental states, as evidenced in the English term "lunatic." In a similar vein, Viator 1935 describes a **tour de lune** as an episode of odd behavior.
Variant: **fou comme la lune.**

couillon comme un bourriquet *(as crazy as a donkey)*
Stupid; foolish; crazy.

couillon comme un cheval *(crazy as a horse)*
Stupid; foolish; crazy.

couillon d'eau douce *(a fresh-water idiot)*
In Louisiana today, the qualifier **d'eau douce** typically distinguishes fresh-water fish from those caught in the sea, and making such a sportsman's distinction when talking about a **couillon**, one of the most derisive epithets a Cajun or Creole can use, adds insult to injury. According to Duneton 1990, though, the qualifier **d'eau douce** has had derogatory connotations in France for a long time. A **marin d'eau douce** *(fresh water sailor)* referred to an inexperienced sailor, and by extension, a boatman on the Seine. As early as the 1600s, an unqualified or ineffective medical doctor in France was known as a **médecin d'eau douce** *(fresh water doctor)*, that is, one who used nothing but plain water in his treatments.

dans les nués *(in the clouds)*
In a dreamworld, not paying attention to reality.

en enfance *(in childhood)*
Senile (of adults).
Variant: **en offense** *(in offense)*.

estropié de la tête *(crippled in the head)*
Crazy; mentally deranged; stupid; foolish.
Variant: **estropié de la cervelle** *(crippled in the brain)*.

faire l'âne pour avoir l'avoine *(to act like a donkey in order to have the oats)*
"To act foolish in order... to reap one's profit" [Viator 1935].
The variant form **faire l'âne pour avoir le foin** *(to act like a donkey in order to have the hay)* is documented by Saucier 1956 in Avoyelles Parish.

fou à baver sus sa chemise *(crazy to the point of drooling on one's shirt)*
Very crazy.
This expression evokes a most graphic and literal image of insanity.

fou à manger de l'herbe *(crazy to the point of eating grass)*
Very crazy.
The expression evokes the image of **les bêtails** *(cattle)* or other hooved creatures.

fou à courir les chemins *(crazy to the point of running in the streets)*.
Very crazy.

fou à sept cylindres *(seven-cylinder crazy)*
Very crazy.
Motors of more than three cylinders typically have even numbers of cylinders. Seven is "one short" or "one too many," odd no matter how it is represented.

fou comme une banane *(as crazy as a banana)*
Very crazy.

fou comme un bâton *(as crazy as a stick)*
Very crazy [PF].

frappé *(struck, slapped)*
Mentally deranged.
Variant: **frappé de la lune** *(moonstruck)*.

fraque
Foolish, silly, not very intelligent.
Said of a woman. The adjective also describes a skittish mare.

pas tout là *(not all there)*
Slightly mentally deranged.
The implication is often that the person is stable enough to live in society, but that it is generally agreed that his mental functions are incapacitated.

pas avoir une bonne idée *(to not have a good mind)*
To be crazy, mentally disturbed [Lanclos 1992].
Note that **bonne idée** in LF can denote either the concept of "good idea" or "good thinking."
Variant: **pas avoir sa bonne idée *(to not have one's good mind)*.**

pas balancé *(unbalanced)*
Mentally unstable.

pas bien plombé *(not well plumbed)*
Mentally deranged; mentally unstable.
Both the notion of something being "out of plumb" (not perfectly perpendicular to the ground) and that of "bad plumbing" (as in leaky pipes) make excellent metaphors for mental instability. The French in France associate lead on the brain metaphorically with serious thinking. In IF, **mettre du plomb dans la tête *(to put lead in one's head)*** means "to reflect seriously" and **n'avoir pas de plomb dans la cervelle *(to have no lead in the brain)*** means "to be intellectually weak." This is rather ironic in light of what we now know about the harmful effects which lead exposure has on mental development.

se jeter à l'eau pour pas se tremper *(to throw oneself into water so as not to get wet)*
To do something foolish which will have worse consequences than the thing one is trying to avoid.

perdre la canique *(to lose the marble)*
To go crazy; "to lose one's marbles" [Beaugh].
Variant: **perdre les caniques *(to lose the marbles)*.**

perdre la carte *(to lose the map/the card)*
To become insane [Calais 1968].

perdre l'équilibre *(to lose one's equilibrium)*
"To do something strange, out of the ordinary, that one should not do" [Calais 1968]; to go crazy.

vitré *(glassy)*
In a daydreaming state; glassy-eyed.

Les hélas et les insultes

Exclamations and Insults

Here is a sampling of words we utter when emotions are high. Though such expressions are often formulaic, they still manage to say a lot about the way French-speaking Louisianians perceive the world around it.

Chapitre 5

avocat! *(lawyer!)*
Know-it-all!

The implication is that lawyers know a lot, and the recipient of such an insult mistakenly thinks he does too. Along those same lines, **ça prend pas un avocat** *(it doesn't take a lawyer)* indicates that something is obvious. DesRuisseaux 1979 reminds us that lawyers and priests were among the few educated people in small villages of long ago, both in Europe and the New World. The European French still use **savant comme un avocat** *(as knowledgeable as a lawyer)* to describe an erudite person.

Bon Dieu seigneur! *(good God the Lord!)*
Expression of surprise, dismay.

The euphemistic **Bon Dieu saignable (good God bleedable)** is sometimes used, probably to avoid further infractions of the second Commandment.

bouche ta gueule! *(stop up your muzzle!)*
Be quiet! Shut up!

Very impolite. In LF, the first consonant sound in **gueule** is usually pronounced like the "j" sound in "judge."

bûche ça à coups de bâton! *(beat that with blows from a stick!)*
I'm so angry about that [BD]!

Variant: **prends ça à coups de bâton!** *(take that with blows from a stick!)*

bûche ça avec une chaîne! *(beat that with a chain!)*
I'm so angry about that [RJG]!

ça, quand-même *(that, anyway)*
As for that!

Expression of disapproval, reproach.

Euphemistic variant: **sac à papier!** *(paper bag).*

c'est l'heure de voir à couper tes culottes! *(it's time to see about cutting your pants!)*
You are acting too impudent; you need to be "put back in your place."

This expression refers to a time when young boys always wore short pants, elevating the wearing of trousers to a symbol of manly behavior.

comment tu crois! *(how do you believe!)*
How do you like that! How about that!

Expression of surprise, often of disapproval. Very common in Evangeline Parish.

fils de putain! *(son of a bitch!)*

Personal insult, expression of pain, anger, or astonishment. Vulgar. According to Duneton 1990, this versatile expletive goes back to 11th century France, in the Old French form **filz a putain**. It has endured here in Louisiana (note that the "s" is not pronounced) and is sometimes heard in the redundant but effective structure **fils de putain de garce** *(roughly, son of a bitching whore)*. Its euphemistic form, **fils de poteau** *(son of a post)*, can be embellished by an additional modifier: **fils de poteau de barrière** *(son of a fencepost)*. It can be used adjectivally, as in **Ce fils de putain de char veut pas partir!** *(That son-of-a-bitching car won't start!)*.

Variants: **fils de garce** *(son of a bitch)*

fils de monstre *(son of a monster)*

jamais de la vie! *(never in my life!)*

Expression of astonishment, disbelief, disapproval.

mais là! *(well there!)*

Expression of astonishment, disapproval.

maîtresse d'école! *(school teacher!)*

Know-it-all!

Like **avocat**, this expression is hurled at those who insist upon showing off their expertise to others. The school mistress would have been one of only a few educated people in small towns of past times.

merci, Bon Dieu! *(thank good God!)*

Expression of relief.

pas de bêtise! (no joke!)

No kidding!

Expression of surprise.

pense donc!/pensez donc! *(think of that!)*

Expression of astonishment, sometimes disapproval.

pitié! *(pity!)*

Expression of astonishment, pity, disapproval.

pour l'amour du Bon Dieu *(for the love of good God!)*

Expression of imploring, exasperation, sometimes astonishment.

Variant: **pour l'amour de Dieu!**

que la Sainte Vierge doit honnir! *(the Holy Virgin must be ashamed!)*

Expression of disapproval.

Sainte Vierge Marie! *(Holy Virgin Mary!)*
Expression of surprise.

sacré bleu! *(sacred blue!)*
Expression of surprise, a euphemism for **sacré Dieu!** *(sacred God!)*.

ta nenaine est caille! *(your godmother is mottled!)*
"That's what you think! You're fooling yourself!" [Calais 1968, Voorhies 1949].

t'es pas maître ici! *(you're not master here!)*
You can't tell me what to do.

t'es pas proche un avocat! *(you're not nearly a lawyer!)*
You're not as smart as you think you are!
See also **avocat!**

ton cul! *(your ass!)*
Says you! Go to hell!
Expression of reproach. Vulgar.

tonnerre m'écrase! *(may thunder strike me down!)*
Like **fils de putain**, this exclamation can indicate anger, pain, or surprise, but it carries the additional weight of being a literal calling for the wrath of God, so a number of people avoid its full force by using the euphemisms **tonnerre mes chiens!** *(thunder my dogs!)*, **tonnerre et z'éclairs!** *(thunder and lightning!)* or simply **tonnerre!**

tristesse! *(sadness)*
Expression of astonishment, pity.

tu crois [que] t'as de la barbe et des crochets! *(you think you have a beard and sideburns!)*
You are impudent!
Addressed to males. Facial hair is, of course, a visible mark of manhood, and the speaker is implying that the behavior of the person being dressed down indicates that he has not yet acquired adult reason.

tu crois [que] t'es maître et majeur! *(you think you are master and major!)*
You think you are behaving like an adult, but you are being foolish or impudent.
This expression would typically be used in addressing a young person. **Maître et majeur** is itself a fixed expression meaning "of age of majority." See also **il est maître et majeur.**

tu vas jamais casser les chaises dans le sénat! *(you'll never break the chairs in the senate!)*
(1) You are not so great as you think you are.
(2) You are not very bright.
(2) You'll never amount to much.

Variant: **tu vas jamais écraser les chaises dans le sénat!** *(You'll never crush the chairs in the senate!)*

va à la merde! *(go to shit)*
Go to hell!

Vulgar. It's probably the most popular way to tell someone off in LF. The one-word expletive form **merde!** is also popular, though in polite company it can be circumvented with the euphemism **mercredi!** *(Wednesday)*.

va donc! *(go on!)*
Expression of disbelief.

va péter à Lacassine! *(go fart in Lacassine!)*
Go away; get out of here.

Lacassine is a small town in remote Jefferson Davis Parish. Though near Lake Charles, the community is considered remote.

va te cacher! *(go hide yourself!)*
Expression of admonition:
(1) I don't believe you!
(2) You should be ashamed of yourself!
(3) Go away and leave me alone!
(4) Go to hell!

va te coucher! *(Go to bed!)*
Expression of admonition:
(1) I don't believe you!
(2) You should be ashamed of yourself!
(3) Go away and leave me alone.
(4) Go to hell!

This expression has been used in France since the 17th century.

The expressions below all follow the same formula, and they are all essentially used as putdowns, either for people found to be arrogant or for people who are not very intelligent . They seem to be most commonly used in direct address to the person being insulted, but they can also be used in referring to a third person, **c'est pas lui/c'est pas elle...***(it's not he / she...).*

c'est pas proche toi le coq de la pinière! *(you are not nearly the cock in the pine grove!)*
You are not so great as you think you are [RS].

c'est pas toi qu'as fait la lune! *(it's not you who made the moon!)*
Note that in oral language in Louisiana, the relative pronoun **qui** tends to elide or contract with forms of the verb **avoir** and some others beginning with vowel sounds.

c'est pas toi qu'as fait la petite almanaque bleue! *(it's not you who made the little blue almanach/calendar!)*

c'est pas toi qu'as fait les allumettes! *(it's not you who made matches!)*

c'est pas toi qu'as inventé la poudre! *(it's not you who invented gunpowder!)*
[Saucier 1956, Reinecke 1971].
This expression is well-known throughout the French-speaking world. The French use the same structure with different "inventions" in a number of common putdowns: **l'eau tiède** *(tepid water)*, **le fil à couper le beurre** *(butter cutter)* [Rey and Chantreau 1979]. In Quebec, an unintelligent person **n'a pas inventé les boutons à quatre trous** *(did not invent four-holed buttons)* [DesRuisseaux 1979].

c'est pas toi qu'as mis l'eau dans le coco! *(it's not you who put water in the coconut!)*
Variant: **c'est pas toi qu'as mis l'eau dans les cocos** *(you're not the one who put water in coconuts)*.

c'est pas toi qu'as pendu la lune! *(it's not you who hung the moon!)*

c'est pas toi qu'as rapé la lune pour faire les étoiles! *(it's not you who grated the moon to make the stars!)*

c'est pas toi qu'as salé la mer! *(it's not you who salted the sea!)*

c'est pas toi qu'es le taureau du côteau! *(it's not you who is the bull on the hill!)*
This expression is also heard in the variant form **le taureau du poteau** *(the bull of the post)*. A man might also defend his territory by saying **c'est moi le taureau du côteau ici!** *(I'm the bull of the hill here!)*.

c'est pas toi qu'étais le premier à péter dessus la lune! *(it's not you who was the first to fart on the moon!)*
Unlike other references to the moon in this group of expressions, which seem almost biblical in their allusion to the Creation story, this one has a distinctly modern theme: space travel! This is a very positive sign of vitality in LF.

Le temps et l'espace
Time and Space

This chapter shows ways to describe one's experiences relative to past and future events, and to distances and areas both large and small.

Chapitre 6

Time:

ça date du temps d'Artaguette *(that dates back to the times of Artaguette)*
(1) That was a long time ago.
(2) It is very old [Buchanan 1931].

ça date de l'an quarante *(that dates back to the year '40)*
(1) That was a long time ago.
(2) It is very old [Buchanan 1931].
In the French-speaking world, the same allusion is found in the expression **s'en moquer comme de l'an quarante (to dismiss as one mocks "the year '40")**, which means to dismiss completely or give no credence to. According to DesRuisseaux 1979, predictions of a day of reckoning were widespread for the year 1740, and afterward the doomsayers were summarily mocked. The same predictions were made for 1840 in both Canada and France.

ça c'était quand Fido était petit *(that was when Fido was small)*
That was a long time ago.
Note that "Fido" is pronounced with a long "i" as in English.

ça c'était quand Caillette était petit veau *(that's when Caillette the cow was a little calf)*
That was a long time ago.
Caillette was a generic nickname, a bit like "Bossy" in English, given to cows which were **de couleur caille *(spotted in color)***. (**La caillette** is also the name of the fourth stomach of a cow.) A variant of this expression, **quand Fido était petit**, may have grown out of the assonant sounds in **Caillette** and **Fido** (pronounced as in English with the long "i" sound). In any case, **Caillette** and her **veau** are popular characters in Louisiana figures of speech. See below.

il doit être après manger du patassa *(he must be eating sunfish)*
He's taking a long time.
Patassa, which refers to several species of sunfish or perch, also known as freshwater bream, is a delicious, but rather small fish with many fine bones. The tedious process of picking out the bones is necessary to avoid choking on them.

Caillette pourrait perdre son veau là-dedans *(Caillette could lose her calf in there)*
The place in question is very messy, disorganized, cluttered.
Mother cows keep very close watch on their young, and only great upheaval of some sort could cause their separation.

il y a bel âge *(it's been a beautiful age)*
It's been a long time.

le temps à Pascal est fini *(Pascal's time is over)*
The times of abundance are over.
Although informants ventured guesses as to the identity of the "Pascal," the original allusion was probably to the Pascal or Easter season, associated with spring, good weather, new growth, etc.

moi, j'étais toujours sous la caca de vache dans ces temps-là *(me, I was still under cow dung in those days)*
I wasn't born yet at that time.

quand les poules auront des dents *(when chickens have teeth)*
Never.
This expression is known throughout the French-speaking world.

un de ces quatre matins *(one of these four mornings)*
One of these days [Saucier 1956].
Although the source did not give a meaning for this expression, one can surmise that it is probably the equivalent of "sooner or later."

tous les tremblements de terre *(every earthquake)*
Every once in a while, infrequently [Lanclos 1992].

Space:

au diable bouilli *(to the devil boiled)*
In a distant and unknown place [Calais 1968].
This expression is still in current use in France.

au large *(out to sea)*
(1) Out on the prairie.
(2) Far away.
A number of nautical terms such as this were adapted by the landlocked prairie dwellers to describe the local terrain. In Southwest Louisiana, the wide expanse of prairie corresponds to the sea, and so **une anse (a cove)** is a wooded area on the prairie.

chien qui va à la chasse perd sa place *(dog who goes hunting loses its place)*
If you leave your place, someone else will usurp it.

Duneton 1990 cites a similar well-known rhyme in France, **qui va à la chasse perd sa place** (without any mention of the dog) as dating back at least to the 19th century.

dans les quatre coins du monde *(in the four corners of the world)*
Everywhere.
The expression, familiar also in France, has its equivalents in English. It recalls a flatter world in which space was conceived of as the quadrants of a square map.
Variants: **dans les quatre coins** *(in the four corners)*,
         dans les quatre paroisses *(in the four parishes)*,
         dans les quatre coins de la paroisse *(in the four corners of the parish)*.

la piste est sèque *(the path is dry)*
No one is there. The place is empty.
Note that in LF the pronunciation of the feminine form of **sec** is identical to masculine.

les finfifonds *(in the deepest, farthest place)*
In a remote place, "the boondocks."
Variant: **les fins-si-fonds**.

il y a un ouragan dans la Chine *(there's a hurricane in China)*
Said to point out that something (a book or picture) is upside down [MBG].

j'ai pas rien perdu à Chicago *(I didn't lose anything in Chicago)*
I don't want to go to Chicago.
The context in which I have heard this expression is usually one in which a person who doesn't like travelling passes up an opportunity to visit a place that is generally considered desirable by others. "Chicago" could be replaced by any place name.

large comme deux doigts *(as wide as two fingers)*
Very narrow.

large comme mes deux fesses *(as large/wide as my two buttocks)*
Very small.
Usually used in reference to a plot of land.

on peut pas y mettre une épingle *(you can't fit a pin there)*
There is no more room; the space in question is very crowded.

un raccourci à défunt Pétain *(the late Pétain's shortcut)*
(1) A supposed shortcut which actually takes longer than the normal route.
(2) An effort which is not worth the trouble.
In variant forms the **raccourci** is sometimes attributed to **Philémon** or some other local character.

tribord et babord *(fore and aft)*
(1) In all directions; on every side.
(2) Inconsistently; in a wavering fashion.

Les riches et les pauvres
The Rich and the Poor

Money isn't everything, as the saying goes, but not having enough of it to meet basic needs makes life a daily struggle. Conversely, fascination with the world of the wealthy is as old as the minting of the first coins. The Cajuns of south Louisiana were traditionally a self-sufficient people, not particularly concerned with amassing wealth themselves. But their language still provides plenty of ways to discuss the subject.

Chapitre 7

à plate *(laid out flat)*
Financially broke; impoverished [LLE].

amarrer ses chiens avec des saucisses *(to use sausages to tie up one's dogs)*
To be abundantly wealthy, so that one can afford excess and foolishness. It can also mean to "tempt fate" or to be "asking for it" in one's imprudent behavior. In France **il attache pas ses chiens avec des saucisses** *(he doesn't tie up his dogs with sausages)*, indicating that a person is stingy, was documented as far back as 1643 [Cellard 1982], but there seems to be no documentable trace in Europe of the affirmative form most common in Louisiana. See also: **il y a plus d'une manière d'étouffer un chien à part lui donner une saucisse.**

au dessus de la farine *(above the flour)*
Rich.

avoir du foin dans ses bottes *(to have hay in one's boots)*
To be wealthy.

avoir la poche pleine *(to have the pocket full)*
To be wealthy.

avoir de l'argent tambour battant *(to have money to "the beat of the drum")*
To be very wealthy.

bien amanché *(well-connected)*
Wealthy.

cacher son argent dans des cornes à boeuf *(to hide one's money in cattle horns)*
To not trust banks; to not save one's money in a bank.

cassé à la chousse *(broken down to the stump)*
Completely broke; financially ruined.
Chousse is a Louisiana variant of **souche** *(tree stump)*, evolved through metathesis, a phenomenon in which sounds that are in close proximity change places. It is sometimes spelled **chouce**.

cassé à la maille *(broken to the "maille")*
Financially devastated [Calais 1968].
According to the *Dictionnaire Hachette*, the **maille** was a coin of extremely small worth under the Capetian dynasty (10th century). It was worth half of a **denier**, which was worth one twelfth of a **sou** *(a cent)*. Compare to **avoir ni sou ni maille** *(to have neither a cent nor a "maille")* in France.

gagner son pain par la sueur de son front *(to earn one's bread by the sweat of one's brow)*
To work hard for a living.

graisser la patte {à quelqu'un} *(to grease {someone's} paw)*
To bribe.
This metaphorical association between grease and money has its roots in 17th century France. It reinforces the image of lubrication being used so that some illicit act can "pass" more easily without question. Rey and Chantreau 1979 cite **graisser le marteau** *(to grease the hammer)* as another French example with the same metaphorical meaning.

se graisser la patte *(to grease one's own paw)*
(1) To accept a bribe.
(2) To make a lot of money by questionable means.
See **graisser la patte**.

il doit à Dieu et ses saints *(he owes to God and His saints)*
He is heavily in debt [Faulk 1977].

les gros dos *(the fat backs)*
Rich people.

pas être à pied *(to not be on foot)*
To be very wealthy.
This understated expression seems clearly to allude to a time when most poor people had no other means of transportation than their two feet, while the wealthy travelled by horseback, carriage, etc.

pauvre comme Job *(as poor as Job)*
Very poor.
This biblical expression is well known in IF.

pauvre comme un rat [d'église] *(as poor as a [church] rat)*
Very poor.
This expression is well known in IF.

riche comme Crésus *(as rich as Croesus)*
Very wealthy.
This expression is used in IF also. According to the *Facts on File Encyclopedia of Word and Phrase Origins*, this expression was popular among the ancient Greeks, whose neighbor, King Croesus of Lydia, was widely considered to be the wealthiest man in the world during the fifth century B.C.

Le malheur et la misère

Misfortune and Misery

Buddhist tradition tells us that if there's one thing we can count on in life, it is suffering. Modern medicine and technology have alleviated much of the misery our ancestors endured, but we can still count on hardship eventually, if we are lucky enough to live so long.

Chapitre 8

à deux doigts de sa mort *(two fingers from death)*
Very close to death [Saucier 1956].

à la guerre comme à la guerre *(at war like at war)*
It's necessary to do without things sometimes [Soileau 1975].

avoir autant de chance qu'un rat dans un tuyau de pipe *(to have as much luck as a rat in a pipe)*
To be unlucky.

avoir du fil à tordre avec {quelqu'un} *(to have thread to twist with {someone})*
To have a lot of difficulty dealing with someone, particularly because of lack of cooperation.
This expression would be typically used in speaking of parents trying to raise an errant child. Dutrieu 1959 notes that the proper spinning of thread by hand, as was the custom in years past, was a technique which required skill and patience. While the expression above describes the sufferer's point of view, the French use **donner du fil à retordre** *(to give thread to twist)* to describe the perpetrator's action. It dates to the 17th century.

avoir pas plus de chance qu'une sauterelle dans un parc de dindes *(to have no more luck than a grasshopper in a turkey pen)*
To be very unlucky.

brasser mer et larmes *(to stir sea and tears)*
To cause misery and trouble; to mess things up.
This is what might be said of a wayward child. A variant form is **brasser mer et par terre** *(to stir up sea and land)*. In IF this motif is found in the expression **chercher par mer et par terre** *(to search by sea and by land)*, which means metaphorically "to search for a long time without getting discouraged."

ça c'est [de la] merde chez Pierre *(it's shit at Pierre's place)*
Now trouble has really begun.
Usually said after a particular event or bit of news is made known.
Variant: **ça c'est merde chez Rodolphe.**

c'est pas baptême catin *(it's not a doll's baptism)*
It's a difficult situation; "it's not fun and games"[Calais 1968].

coller {quelqu'un} à {faire quelque chose} *(to stick {someone doing something})*
To catch someone in the act of doing something.

couper l'herbe {à quelqu'un} (*to cut {someone's} grass*)
To take away one's chance of succeeding [Saucier 1956].

cuisses cailles a passé (*mottled thighs has come by*)
Nothing has been going right.
Cuisses Cailles is a nickname for the devil, often associated with ill fortune or bad luck.

fais-toi pas une gomme avec ça (*don't make yourself a gum with that*)
Don't get your hopes up; don't rely on this happening.

être la nenaine {à quelqu'un} (*to be {someone's} godmother*)
To be someone's hard luck.

être maître et majeur (*to be master and major*)
He's an adult, old enough to be responsible for his own actions.
This expression of resignation is typically offered to distraught parents. Though I could find no French ancestor to this expression, 20th century French colloquial language includes **être majeur et vacciné (*to be of age and vaccinated*)**, meaning "to be responsible for one's actions."

être sus le mouroir (*to be on the deathbed/deathplace*)
To be on the point of death [Parr 1940].

être venu un fil de sa mort (*to come a thread from death*)
To come very close to dying; to almost die.
Variants: **être venu un cheveu de sa mort (*to come a hair from death*)**
   être venu deux cheveux de sa mort (*to have come two hairs from one's death*) [Saucier 1956].

flambé (*roasted on a flame*)
Out of a luck; a failure.

il était pas aux noces (*he was not at the wedding*)
(1) He was in an uncomfortable or disagreable situation.
(2) He doesn't know what he's talking about.
Duneton 1990 cites meaning (1) for this expression as early as the 19th century in France. In at least two variants, the groom's name is used: **il était pas aux noces à Lézime**
   il était pas aux noces à Norbert.

là, la merde est pris! (*now the shit has taken off!*)
Now the trouble has begun; it has "hit the fan."

manger de la misère *(to eat misery)*
To have a lot of trouble and hardship in one's life [Lanclos 1992].
Variant: **passer de la misère *(to go through misery)*** [OT].

manger le pain blanc en premier *(to eat the white bread first)*
(1) To have the easy life first, usually followed by some hardship.
(2) To take the best of something first without consideration for
others [PNA].
Though today's concerns about health and nutrition have reversed values about the
relative merits of brown and white bread, this expression tenaciously recalls a time
when white flour was reserved for the privileged. According to Duneton 1990, meaning
(1) dates back to the early 1500s in France.

manger le poisson d'avril *(to eat the April Fish)*
To be tricked on April Fool's Day.
In France, the fish is the definitive symbol of April Fool's Day. Children amuse
themselves on that day by attaching paper fish cutouts to the backs of unsuspecting
playmates, and bakeries sell fish-shaped pastries to celebrate the occasion. It is
interesting that the fish is preserved in this LF expression, even though no other
Louisiana observance of April Fool's Day includes that symbol.

manquer le bateau avec le tiquette dans la main *(to miss the boat with one's ticket in one's hand)*
To miss a good opportunity [Lanclos 1992].
Variant: **manquer le char avec le tiquette dans la main *(to miss the train with one's ticket in hand)*.**

passer du bleu de ciel avec {quelqu'un} *(to go through the blue of the sky with {someone})*
To suffer misery, a hard time with someone [HD].
Informants cited dealing with a difficult or troubled child as an example. The related
expression **voir [du] bleu *(to see blue)*** can be used, without reference to a person as
the cause, to mean simply "to endure intense suffering". Note: In LF, the infinitive form
"souffert," pronounced "soo-fair," is more common than the IF **"souffrir."**
Variant: **souffert du bleu de ciel avec {quelqu'un} *(to suffer the blue of the sky with {someone})*.**

poisson à terre sèque *(a fish on dry land)*
One who has no luck; one who is lost [Simon 1991].
Note that in LF the pronunciation of the feminine form of **sec** is identical to masculine.

rabourer à travers les rangs *(to plow across the rows)*
To do things the hard way; to make things hard for oneself [BA].
Note that **rabourer** is from the IF **labourer**. The "l" and "r" sounds in LF are formed in similar positions in the mouth, and this same assimilation occurs with other LF words such as **rougarou (loupgarou IF)** and **carculer (calculer IF)**.

ramasser dans les rangs hauts *(to pick in the high rows)*
To have it easy [BA].

s'en passer au bout du bec *(to pass up something at the tip of one's beak)*
To not get or not have any of something [Simon 1991].

si c'est pas les maringouins, c'est les chouboulures *(if it's not the mosquitoes, it's the prickly heat)*
Nothing is perfect; there's always some kind of problem or difficulty; "if it's not one thing, it's another."

si on peut pas téter maman, il faut téter memère *(if one can't suckle Mama, one suckles Grandma)*
You take what you can get; you have to make the best of bad situation [Lanclos 1992].

suer comme un bâtard à une réunion de famille *(to sweat like a bastard at a family reunion)*
(1) To sweat profusely.
(2) To be in a very awkward or uncomfortable situation.

suer comme un nègre à la messe *(to sweat like a Negro at Mass)*
(1) To sweat profusely.
(2) To be in a very awkward or uncomfortable situation.

suer des carvelles *(to sweat large nails)*
To have a lot of difficulty doing something [Saucier 1956].

suer les Ponce Pilate *(to sweat Pontius Pilates)*
(1) To sweat profusely.
(2) To be in a very awkward or uncomfortable situation.

tirer la courte paille *(to draw the short straw)*
To have a hard life [Saucier 1956].

tirer une patate chaude {à quelqu'un} *(to throw a hot potato {at someone})*
(1) To pose a difficult problem to someone.
(2) To put someone on the spot [PNA].

vivre en espoir et mourir comme un vieux chien *(to live in hope and die like an old dog)*
To have a miserable life [TBN].

voir [du] bleu *(to see blue)*
To endure suffering.

Le manger et la boisson
Food and Drink

The foods one identifies with a culture are its most recognized and probably its most enduring features. The fact that this chapter includes no fewer than six ways to describe bad coffee, for example, is certainly indicative of the value we place on a good, strong and very black cup of the brew.

baigne (n.m.)
A corn or wheat cake fried in deep fat [Daigle 1934].

baptiser *(to baptise)*
To dilute; to add water to (a drink such as wine or coffee).
The expression alludes to the pouring of water over a baby's head during the baptismal rite.

bécassine créole *(Creole snipe)*
Red beans and rice [Reinecke 1971].

bomme à café (n.f.) *(coffee "bomb")*
Coffee pot [Babin 1937].
The spelling is the informant's, rendering the local pronunciation of **bombe***. In Southeastern Louisiana,* **une bombe** *is a generic name for a non-cast iron pot, whereas the rest of the state uses either* **bombe** *(or* **bouilloire***) to refer to a water kettle. In IF,* **bombe** *can refer to something spherical, such as a scoop of ice cream. The use of this expression to mean "coffee pot" in Lafourche seems therefore to be an extension of its reference to pots.*

bomme queue raide *(straight-tailed "bomb")*
Large pot [Babin 1937].
See comments for **bomme à café***. The "straight tail" probably refers to the pot handle.*

chaud-l'eau (n.m.) *(hot water)*
Weak coffee [Parr 1940].
In the original source, the entry was spelled phonetically **chau-lau***.*

estomac de mulâtre *(mulatto stomach)*
Stage Plank cookie.
This was the name of a popular gingerbread cookie, widely available in South Louisiana grocery stores until recent years. They were typically rectangular in shape and covered with pink icing.

lavure (n.f.) *(dishwater/slop water)*
Bad coffee or soup [Calais 1968].

nanane (n.m.)
Food (in babytalk) [Olivier 1937].

orteil de nègre *(Negro toe)*
Black walnut [Granier 1939].

pet de nonne *(nun's fart)*
Cream puff [PNA].
This expression is widely used in the French-speaking world.

pichette (n.f.)
Weak coffee [Calais 1968].

pissat de chatte (cat urine)
Bad coffee.

pop rouge *(red "pop")*
Strawberry soft drink.
Note that in South Louisiana, "soda" usually refers to an ice cream-based drink. Carbonated beverages are commonly referred to as "pop" in this area, both in English and in French.

prendre un bossal *(to take a halter)*
"To give oneself a treat; to eat something nice" [Hickman 1940].
The term **bossal** is borrowed from the Spanish **bozal**, meaning "muzzle."

quarante-quatre *(forty-four)*
Red bean [Hurst 1938].

tafia (m.s.) *(tafia)*
Bad-tasting coffee [Brandon 1955].
Literally speaking, **tafia** was a low-quality form of rum.

une tasse de pissat chaud *(a cup of hot urine)*
Weak coffee [PNA].

toto
Cake (in child's vocabulary) [Olivier 1937, Guilbeau 1950].

yeast macaque
Parrot and Monkey brand baking powder [Olivier 1937].

Le corps et la santé
Body and Health

This chapter includes ways of describing the delicate and not-so-delicate functions and phenomena of our physical selves. Though some entries would be considered crude or even cruel, they reflect the language as it is or has been spoken by a wide spectrum of the population. The list includes descriptive expressions for infirmities and defects, as well as expressions of appreciation and admiration.

Chapitre 10

avoir des fesses de moiselle *(to have mosquitohawk buttocks)*
To have thin buttocks, a skinny behind.
Typically derogatory. The term **moiselle** is from **demoiselle**, the common name in IF for "damselfly." In Louisiana, the term **moiselle** has expanded to become the generic name for any dragonfly-like insect. In some areas, the mosquitohawk (as dragonflies are called in Louisiana) is known as a **cigale**, and the term **cigale de bois** is used to refer to cicadas.

avoir des jambes de baguettes *(to have stick legs)*
To have thin legs [PF].
Variant: **avoir des jambes comme des baguettes** *(to have legs like sticks)*.

avoir des jambes comme des baguettes de coton *(to have legs like cotton branches)*
To have thin legs [FBL].

avoir des jambes comme des baguettes de fusil *(to have legs like rifle barrels)*
To have thin legs.

avoir des jambes comme des globes de lampe *(to have legs like lamp globes)*
(1) To have big legs [FBL].
(2) To have shapely legs (of a woman) [PF].

avoir des jambes comme des pattes de moqueur *(to have mockingbird legs)*
To have thin legs [PF].

avoir des oreilles comme un pot de chambre *(to have ears like a chamber pot)*
To have big ears [BL].

avoir des oreilles comme un taxi avec les deux portes ouvertes *(to have ears like a taxi with both doors open)*
To have big ears.
This gem was heard in Evangeline Parish.

avoir des oreilles d'éléphant *(to have elephant ears)*
To have big ears.

avoir des oreilles de tayaut *(to have hound dog ears)*
To have big ears.

avoir faim comme un chien *(to be as hungry as a dog)*
To be very hungry.

avoir la fale basse *(to have the craw low)*
To be hungry.
Le Glossaire du parler français au Canada tells us that this expression has the same meaning in French Canada, while the *Practical Handbook of Québec and Acadian French* gives "to feel very tired or depressed" as its meaning there. *Le Glossaire* tells us that the term **fale** has its roots in the dialect of Normandy, where **avoir la fale basse** means figuratively "to have a hard time making a living."

avoir la fale pleine *(to have the craw full)*
To have eaten enough; to be "full."

avoir la fritche
To have diarrhea.
The "proper" euphemistic term for diarrhea in LF is **le dérangement.**

avoir la queue sur le dos *(to have one's tail on one's back)*
To be on the go.
Variant: **avoir la queue sus le dos.**

avoir la vavite *(to have the "go-quick")*
To have diarrhea.
The "proper" euphemistic term for diarrhea in LF is **le dérangement.**

avoir la vie dans sa main *(to have life in one's hand)*
To almost die [Brandon 1955].

avoir le "flag" *(to have the flag)*
To menstruate.

avoir le tour d'âge *(to have the turn of age)*
To go through menopause.

avoir les foies blancs *(to have lungs)*
To be long-lived; "said of a woman who has survived two or more husbands" [Hickman 1940].
Though **foie** usually refers to the *liver* in French, **les foies blancs** in a number of dialects in France, as well as in Louisiana, are *the lungs*. Could it be that lungs symbolize endurance or hardiness? In France as early as 1883, this same expression was documented to mean "to be afraid, to lack courage," and even the ancient Greeks had a direct translation of this same expression to describe a fearful person.

avoir les yeux dolents *(to have doleful eyes)*
To appear sleepy.
Variant: **avoir les yeux de long** *(to have long eyes)*.

avoir les yeux égarés *(to have "straying" eyes)*
To appear tired.

avoir les yeux gouaires *(to have pale eyes)*
To have a blank look [LO].
Gouaire is from the Spanish **güero**, meaning "blond" or "very pale."

avoir les yeux noirs comme des socos *(to have eyes as black as muscadines)*
To have very dark eyes.
Variant: **avoir des yeux de soco**. The ripe muscadine grape recalls not only the color, but also the large, round shape that is stereotypical of Cajun eyes.

avoir l'oeil au bois *(to have an eye toward the woods)*
To be cock-eyed.
See also **avoir un oeil qui dit merde à l'autre**.

avoir un crapaud dans la gorge *(to have a toad in the throat)*
To be hoarse.

avoir un oeil qui dit merde à l'autre *(to have one eye that says "shit" to the other)*
To be cock-eyed.
Attested as early as 1878 in France, this expression is based on the image of two eyes angry with each other, in which one "turns away." In France, one might also hear **avoir un oeil qui joue au billard et l'autre qui compte les points** *(to have one eye which plays pool while the other counts the points)* [Duneton 1990].

avoir un oeil qui gagne chez Nonc Pierre *(to have one eye heading toward Uncle Pierre's)*
To be cock-eyed.
See also **avoir un oeil qui dit merde à l'autre**.

avoir un nez comme un bec *(to have a nose like a beak)*
To have a long, pointed nose.

avoir un nez comme un bec à lancette *(to have a nose like an anhinga)*
To have a long, pointed nose.

avoir un nez de manche de pompe *(to have a nose like a pump handle)*
To have a long, pointed nose.

avoir une quille *(to have a bowling pin)*
To have a big nose.

babiche (n.f.) *(rawhide)*
Energy.
See also **fait du nerf et de la babiche**. *The sense of* **babiche** *as "rawhide" is known in Canada. According to the* Trésor de la Langue Française, *its origins are in the Micmac word* **ababich**, *meaning "rope" or "cord."*

boscot (m.)/boscotte (f.)
A hunch-backed person.

boulette (n.f.) du genou *(the knee-ball)*
Knee-cap.

caouenne (n.f.)*(turtle)*
Vagina.
The word is of Caribbean origin, from the Carib indigenous language, and means "sea turtle," Indeed, in some areas of Louisiana such as Evangeline and Lafourche Parishes, its literal meaning is the only one known. However, Louisianians from areas where only the figurative meaning is known have been at times shocked and offended to leave their dialectal area and find themselves invited to eat **une sauce piquante de caouenne** *(turtle peppery stew)*.

ses cheveux sont tous chien-fou *(his/hair is all dog-crazy)*
His/her hair is disheveled [Reinecke 1971].

cocotte (n.f.)
Vagina.
French visitors in South Louisiana have innocently caused the embarrassment and confusion of their hosts by referring (as they do in France) to cooking pots as **cocottes**.

combouille (n.f.)
Toe cheese [Olivier 1937].
The spelling here is Olivier's, but since LF speakers don't always distinguish between the pronunciation of "om" and "am," it seems likely that this term is derived from the French **cambouis**, *which refers both to old axle grease and to the residue found in the areas where a horse's skin comes in contact with the leather of its harness during a workout. Olivier 1937 also gives the verb* **décombouiller** *as meaning* **to clean**.

comme ça *(like that)*
Pregnant [Reinecke 1971].

couver un rhume *(to be incubating a cold)*
To be catching a cold.
The verb **couver** typically is used in the context of fowl and their setting upon eggs in order to hatch them.

crapaud [de nez] *(nose toad)*
Crusty nasal excretion; a "booger."

deux pouces de jambe et le cul tout de suite *(two inches of leg and the ass right next)*
A humorous way of referring to a very short person.
Note that in LF, **cul** usually pronounced something like the English word "chew" in Louisiana.

dormir debout *(to sleep standing up)*
To be very tired.

en ceinture *(belted)*
Pregnant [Hickman 1940, Ditchy 1932].
Terrebonne Parish residents were familiar with the variant **en pleine ceinture** *(in full pregnancy)* [LLE]. The IF **enceinte** *(pregnant)*, has its origins in the same root word.

en famille *(in family)*
Pregnant.
This euphemism is quite common and corresponds to the English euphemism "to be in the family way." It is used colloquially in many French-speaking countries.

faire du lard *(to make lard)*
To get fat [Viator 1935].
In France, this same expression has been used since the early 1600s to mean "to sleep a long time" [Duneton 1990].

galette (n.f.)
Vagina.
In France, a **galette** is a flat, round cookie, or a buckwheat pancake. Obviously, the possibilities for bewilderment and embarrassment are myriad when French tourists visit Louisiana and unwittingly use this term as they would in France.

hors d'âge *(beyond age)*
Very old; too old to work (Pirkle 1935, Calais 1968).

jambe de lait *(milk leg)*
Thrombophlebitis, the medical condition known commonly as
"varicose veins."

il faut qu'il se tourne pour faire un ombrage *(he has to turn
[sideways] to make a shadow)*
He is very thin.
The shadow motif for describing thinness has several variants: **Il faut qu'il se lève
deux fois pour faire un ombrage** *(He has to stand up twice to make a shadow)*
and from humorist Marion Marcotte, **il faut qu'elle marche deux fois à la même
place pour faire un ombrage** *(She has to walk twice in the same place to make
a shadow)*.

membré comme une tortue de rosée *(built like a dew turtle)*
Husky; muscular [PF].

L'action et l'inertie

Action and Inertia

This chapter could have been entitled "to do or not to do." It includes a wide variety of ways to describe activity and inactivity in the course of our everyday lives.

Sleeping:

à la paille *(to/on the straw)*
To bed; in bed [Trahan 1936].
*Only prepositions make the distinction here between poverty, **sur la paille (poor)** and repose. In Louisiana, the "straw" referred to in this expression would have served as stuffing for a mattress, commonly known as a **paillasse**. I was unable to document the use of **à la paille** in IF, though **sur la paille** is used in France to mean "in bed."*

le bouchon est après caler *(the cork is bobbing)*
Someone is nodding off to sleep [OV].

calibossé (adj.)
(1) Said of one who goes to bed early [Guilbeau 1950].
(2) Badly dressed [JJG].
*Variant: **caillebossé**.*

cogner des clous *(to hammer nails)*
To nod off while trying to avoid sleep.

dormir comme une caille molle *(to sleep like a soft-shelled turtle)*
To sleep soundly [PNA].

dormir comme un caïman *(to sleep like an alligator)*
To sleep soundly [Calais 1968].
*The co-existance of this expression and the previously listed **dormir comme une caille molle** is probably due in part to the similarity of their pronunciation.*

dormir comme un congo *(to sleep like a water mocassin)*
To sleep soundly.

dormir comme une bûche *(to sleep like a log)*
To sleep well.
*The English-influenced **dormir comme un "log"** was mentioned by several recent informants and was even documented in some of the older collections from the 30s and 40s.*

être dans le Paris des oies *(to be in the Paris of geese)*
To be in deep sleep [Parr 1940].

faire la grasse matinée *(to do the fat morning)*
To sleep late.

The adjective **grasse** in this context functions like the **gras** in **Mardi Gras**, a time of self-indulgence and plenty. The expression is quite popular today throughout the French-speaking world, though its origins, according to Duneton 1990, are in the late 1400s.

faire le congo *(to act like a water mocassin)*
To pretend to be sleeping [Faulk 1977].

faire singo
To take a nap [Calais 1968].

frapper un noeud *(to hit a knot)*
To make a snorting sound when snoring [JRG].
Thematically related to **cogner des clous (to hammer nails)**, this expression evokes the disturbance caused when hammering into wood is hindered by coming upon a knot.

passer la nuit blanche *(to spend a white night)*
To not sleep all night, typically against one's will.
Duneton 1990 explains that this expression has its origins in the extravagant fireworks displays given in the course of all-night parties hosted at one time by certain people of means in France. These were commonly called **nuits blanches**, referring to the brilliantly lit skies produced. By the beginning of the 19th century, the figurative meaning, "a night without sleep," had passed into popular language, where it remains today.

passer une nuit à la plaille *(to spend a night on the beach)*
To spend a sleepless night [Guilbeau 1950].
This is a regional expression, as the word **plaille** is typically associated with the Bayou Lafourche dialect.

pêcher *(to fish)*
To nod off in trying to avoid sleep [OV].
This expression is in the same thematic family as **le bouchon est après caler** mentioned above.

Helping and hindering:

donner un coup de main {à quelqu'un} *(to give {someone} a hand)*
To assist someone in doing something.
Traditionally referring to physical work, the **coup de main** could also refer to an event, similar to a barn raising, in which a group of friends gathered to help someone construct a building or carry out some large-scale task such as a hog butchering. This also typically involved sharing a meal and a festive atmosphere.

donner un pied {à quelqu'un} *(to give a foot {to someone})*
To give someone an advantage, "a foot up" [Saucier 1956].

donner une partance {à quelqu'un} *(to give {someone} a "start")*
To help someone start a venture [ABR].
Literally speaking, a **partance** usually consisted of seeds or bread yeast passed from one person to another.

faire une belle grâce {à quelqu'un} *(to do a beautiful grace {to someone})*
To do someone a good turn, a favor.

fouille-merde (n.f.) *(dung-beetle)*
(1) A meddler.
(2) One who touches things too readily.
Literally, the verb **fouiller** means "to dig or excavate," while **merde** is, of course, a less refined way to refer to "dung."

fourrer le doigt partout *(to stick one's finger everywhere)*
To meddle in the affairs of others.
Variant: **fourrer le nez partout** *(to stick one's nose everywhere)*

mettre des bâtons dans la roue *(to put sticks in the wheel)*
To put impediments or obtacles in the way of one's success.
Variant: **mettre des bâtons dans les roues** *(to put sticks in the wheels)*

mettre l'épaule à la roue *(to put one's shoulder to the wheel)*
(1) To help.
(2) To get to work.

mettre le pied dans la boue *(to put one's foot in the mud)*
To do something which could have bad consequences [Lanclos 1992].

mettre son nez dans le bol *(to put one's nose in the bowl)*
To interfere [Parr 1940].
Though this expression was confirmed by a number of contemporary informants, most report **bol** as a feminine noun in LF.

Using words:

à haute tête *(high-headed)*
Out loud [EB].

à pleine tête *(full-headed)*
Out loud [EB].

battre sa gueule *(to beat one's muzzle)*
To chatter on; to talk excessively.
In LF, the first consonant sound in **gueule** is usually pronounced like the "j" sound in "judge." **Ferme ta gueule!** is a typical, if not very cordial, way of telling someone to quit talking.

fermer son grabot *(to close one's cotton boll)*
To stop talking; to close one's mouth.

mettre le bogui avant le cheval *(to put the buggy before the horse)*
(In telling a story) to recount the events in the wrong order [Simon 1991].

monter sa manivelle *(to turn one's crank)*
To get "wound up" as one begins talking [Viator 1935].

parler comme du tactac *(to talk like popcorn)*
To speak in a rapid, staccato fashion.

pas avoir la langue dans la poche *(to not have one's tongue in one's pocket)*
(1) To talk a lot.
(2) To not be embarrassed to speak.
(3) To be outspoken.

pas avoir la langue d'amarrée *(to not have one's tongue tied)*
To be a big talker.

pas mettre des gants *(to not put on gloves)*
To speak directly and plainly, even at the risk of offending another; to "not mince words."

poser sa chique [et faire le mort] *(to put down one's chaw [and play dead])*
To keep silent; to "hold one's tongue" [Hickman 1940, Voorhies 1949].
In IF, **poser sa chique** *means metaphorically "to die"* [Rey and Chantreau 1979].

pousser {quelqu'un} dans les rangs courts *(to push {someone} in the low rows)*
To force someone through argument to say or admit something [BA].

Moving:

courir le perron *(to run the porch)*
To run the roads; to run around a lot [HP].

danser avec elle, c'est comme traîner une herse dans les grandes herbes *(dancing with her is like dragging a harrow in tall grass)*
She is a terrible dancer; she cannot follow when dancing [PBT].

danser la queue raide *(to dance with the tail straight)*
To dance very energetically; to "cut a rug" [RRL].
According to the informant, the tail in question here seems to be one's shirt or coat tail, which would be flying straight out if one were spinning very fast.

faire chaudière *(to make cookpot)*
To camp; to halt overnight [Hickman 1940].

faire le cochon de St. Antoine *(to act like St. Anthony's pig)*
To roam around from place to place [Parr 1940].

fendre l'air *(to split the air)*
To get away very quickly.

ficher le camp *(to leave the camp)*
To leave.
This expression is used among French speakers worldwide.

foutre le camp *(to leave the camp)*
To go away.
This expression is well known in IF.

galoper comme un chat échaudé *(to run like a scalded cat)*
To get out fast from a trap or a difficult situation [FP].

grouiller son casaquin *(to move one's blouse IF)*
To hurry up [Buchanan 1931].
The word **casaquin** is an old French reference to a woman's blouse. Though considered archaic in IF, it now refers metaphorically to the body, in the expression above as well as the IF **sauter sur le casaquin de quelqu'un**, which means "to jump on or beat up someone."

haler ses fesses *(to haul one's buttocks)*
To leave, usually quickly.
The verb **haler,** which is restricted to maritime language in IF, is the common LF term for "to pull" or "to haul."
Variants: **haler son cul** *(to haul one's ass),*
  haler son derrière *(to haul one's behind).*

haler ses frètes *(to haul one's freight)*
To leave quickly [TBB].
Variant: **haler son frète** [Coco 1933, Calais 1968].

haler son gratin *(to haul one's crust)*
To get away quickly [Coco 1933].

lever la queue *(to raise one's tail)*
To make a quick getaway [Viator 1935].

lever le pied *(to raise one's foot)*
To leave [Saucier 1956].

partir avant les guêpes *(to leave before the wasps)*
To leave early.

partir marron *(to leave as a fugitive)*
(1) To escape, to flee.
(2) To leave without informing anyone.
The term **marron** is from Caribbean Spanish adjective **cimarrón** used to describe a fugitive slave.
Variant: **partir en marron** [Coco 1933].

partir mors aux dents *(to leave with the bit in one's mouth)*
To bolt suddenly [Deblanc 1935].

pas aller par les quatre chemins *(to not go by way of the four roads)*
To go directly to one's goal [Saucier 1956].

pas [se] traîner les pattes *(to not drag one's paws/feet)*
To go quickly; to do something quickly without wasting time.
Variants: **pas traîner les pieds** *(feet)*
        pas traîner les talons *(heels)* [HD]

ses pieds touchaient ses fesses *(his/her feet touched his/her buttocks)*
He/she was running very fast.

tamiser (v.i.) *(to sift)*
"To shake while dancing in such a way that the whole body trembles" [Coco 1933].

tourner casaque *(to turn coat)*
To flee; to run away.
According to Dutrieu 1957, the term probably dates back to the religious wars of the Reformation in France, where **casaque** was the overgarment worn by soldiers. Those who wanted to abandon service or change sides in the conflict were careful to turn their coats inside out to hide their origins. In contemporary France, the term can also mean "to change sides in a dispute."

Human interaction:

faire des ricracs *(to make rickrack)*
To do something in order to create a good impression [LO].

faire un chapelet {à quelqu'un} *(to say a rosary {for someone})*
To tell someone off.

jeter de l'huile sur le feu *(to throw oil on the fire)*
To excite or encourage (usually a conflict or scandal).

mettre la puce à l'oreille {à quelqu'un} *(to put the flea to the ear {of someone})*
(1) To hint or suggest to someone.
(2) To warn someone subtly about a danger.
(3) To make one suspicious by one's words.
This expression is well-known in IF.

mettre le feu à la paille *(to start the straw on fire)*
To start or add to the momentum of a rumor or conflict by one's words.
Saucier mentions **un feu de paille** *(a straw fire)* in her collection to mean "something which does not last."
Variants: **mettre le feu à la poudre** *(to start the gunpowder on fire)* [Saucier 1956]
        mettre le feu à la paillasse *(to start the mattress on fire)*

[se] noyer dans son [propre] crachat *(to drown in one's own spittle)*
(1) To talk on without getting to the point.
(2) To talk too much.
(3) To be unable to speak because one has forgotten what one wanted to say.

Since George Reineke is one of the sources for this expression, it's reasonable to assume that it was known in New Orleans French and probably in France. The related expression **avoir peur de se noyer dans son propre crachat *(to be afraid of drowning in one's own spittle)*** *means "to be afraid to undertake ventures, to take chances."*

Wasting time:

cracher dans le feu *(to spit in the fire)*
To do something useless; to waste one's time [TBB].

mouliner la queue du chien *(to mill the dog's tail)*
To procrastinate.

The image evoked in this expression is that of someone turning a dog's tail the way he might a sifter or an old time coffee mill. In ellipsis, the verb **mouliner** *was also used alone to mean "to procrastinate."*
Variant: **tournailler la queue du chien *(to turn the dog's tail)***

mettre de la boucane en sac *(to put smoke in a sack)*
To do a task which serves no purpose [Lanclos 1992].

siffler dans le vent *(to whistle in the wind)*
To do something useless; to waste one's time [PNA].

tâtonner (v.i.) *(to grope/feel one's way around)*
(1) To waste time.
(2) To procrastinate [HP].
The reflexive form **se tâtonner** *means "to pet," as in love-making [RJG].*

Other:

avoir une figure comme une vache qu'a soif *(to have a face like a thirsty cow)*
To grimace; to show displeasure or disapproval in one's facial expressions [PBT].

brailler à chaudes larmes *(to cry hot tears)*
(1) To cry wholeheartedly, profusely.
(2) To cry out loud.
Variants: **brailler à haute tête** [EB]
         brailler à haute voix [MBG]

brailler comme un petit bébé
To cry profusely.

se casser en deux *(to break oneself in two)*
To strive hard to do something [LO].

chanter comme un carencro *(to sing like a buzzard)*
To sing badly.

coucher au serein *(to sleep in the dew)*
To stay out all night, usually after having caroused.
One might presumably end up waking to find oneself lying outside in the morning dew
after an all night escapade.

étendre la bête *(to extend the beast)*
To urinate.

faire de l'eau *(to make water)*
To urinate.

faire des papillotes *(to make "curls")*
"To do fancy acrobatic tricks" [Viator 1935].

faire la culbute *(to do a cartwheel)*
To give birth [Hickman 1940].
Variant: **faire des culbutes** *(to do cartwheels).*

faire son mulet *(to act like a mule)*
To yawn [Hurst 1938].

flamber les yeux *(to flame the eyes)*
To stare with curiosity [Olivier 1937].

grandir comme un pied de chou *(to grow like a cabbage plant)*
To grow up quickly [OT].

mettre du fond de la malle *(to put on from the bottom of the trunk)*
To get dressed up; to put on one's fine clothes [MD].
Clothing from the bottom of the trunk would have been one's finer things that were not worn very often.

planter chêne *(to plant oak)*
(1) To stand on one's head.
(2) To fall forward on one's head.

plomber (v.t.) *(to plumb)*
To kill by shooting [Jeansonne 1938]; to "fill with lead."
The noun **plomb** means "lead." The verb form **plomber** originally referred to using a piece of lead attached to a string to check the depth of water or measure whether a structure is straight up or down.

se tenir comme un gris-gris *(to hold on to one another like a spell)*
To hold on very tightly to one another [Guilbeau 1950].

tirer avec la mire fine *(to fire with a fine aim)*
To be precise in one's work or skill [PNA].

tirer une poignette *(to pull a "fistfull")*
To masturbate (of men).
La poignette is the act of masturbation. The French used the related form **poignet**, as in **jouer au poignet (to masturbate). La veuve poignet** referred to the act in noun form [Duneton 1990].
Variant: **haler une poignette.**

tomber dans les fesses à Black *(to fall in Black's buttocks)*
To faint [Saucier 1956].

tomber en confiture *(to fall in jelly)*
To faint [Guilbeau 1950].

L'intelligence et le manque d'esprit
Intelligence and the Lack Thereof

How is it that our intolerance for the foolishness of others seems to inspire such witty, even poetic, figures of speech? This chapter includes expressions for intelligence as well as stupidity, but those describing the latter are in the vast majority.

Chapitre 12

afilé (adj.) *(sharpened)*
Smart; often sneaky.
Variant: **enfilé**

**apprendre [par coeur] comme un perroquet *(to learn [by heart]
like a parrot)***
To learn quickly, easily.

aussi bête que la lune est haute *(as stupid as the moon is high)*
Very stupid.
Comparison to the height of the moon to show an extreme can be found in several LF
figures of speech.

avoir bonne idée *(to have good idea)*
To be intelligent; to be a good thinker.
Idée in LF can mean both "idea" and "mind."
Variant: **avoir sa bonne idée *(to have one's good idea)*.**

avoir le nez long *(to have a long nose)*
To be wise, informed; to know everything [Parr 1940].

**avoir pas plus d'à peu près qu'une truie aux socos *(to not have
more sense that a sow in a muscadines)***
To not have good judgement, good sense [PF].
Some informants used **à propos** instead of **à peu près**.

baroque
Stupid [Granier 1939].

bétaille *(animal)*
Stupid [Granier 1939].

The use of the word **bête** *to describe lack of intelligence is so firmly
ensconced in popular language that we tend to forget its link with its
original meaning, "animal." The most amusing figures of speech using
the term are those that subtly remind us of this connection.*

bête à coucher dehors *(stupid to the point of sleeping outside)*
Very stupid.

bête à manger de l'herbe *(stupid to the point of eating grass)*
Very stupid.
The French say **bête à manger des chardons *(thistles)*** and more commonly **bête à
manger du foin *(hay)*** [Rey-Chantreau 1979].

bête à pincer l'herbe *(stupid to the point of pinching grass)*
Very stupid.

ça c'est assez bête, si ça tombe à quatre pattes ça va pas avoir assez d'esprit pour se lever *(that [person] is so stupid, if he falls on all fours, he won't have enough sense to get up)*
That person is very stupid.

c'est assez bête, ça pourrait se mettre à quatre pattes et manger de l'herbe *(that [person] is so stupid he could get on all fours and eat grass)*
That person is very stupid.

bête comme ses [deux] pieds *(as stupid as one's [two] feet)*
Very stupid.

bête comme un bourriquet *(as stupid as a donkey)*
Very stupid.

bête comme un cabri *(as stupid as a goat)*
Very stupid.

bête comme un cheval *(as stupid as a horse)*
Very stupid.

bête comme un chou *(as stupid as a cabbage)*
Very stupid [Brandon 1955].

bête comme un poteau de coin *(as stupid as a corner post)*
Very stupid.

bête comme une bête à cornes *(as stupid as a horned animal)*
Very stupid.
Bête à cornes typically refers to cattle in LF.

bête comme une cruche *(as stupid as a jar)*
Very stupid.

bête comme une djogue *(as stupid as a jug)*
Very stupid.

bête comme une [z']oie *(as stupid as a goose)*
Very stupid.
A foolish person might simply be called **une [z']oie**.

bigote (adj. m./f.)
Stupid [Parr 1940].

biocque
Foolish; not intelligent [Trahan 1936].

braque (adj.) *(short-haired pointer; a type of dog)*
Stupid [Jeansonne 1938].
The metaphorical use of **braque** as "crazy" is also common in France.

ça c'est la grande calebasse! *(that's the big gourd!)*
What a fool! [Daigle 1934].
Calebasse often refers metaphorically to the head.

chiqueur de lavettes grasses *(a chewer of soapy dishrags)*
A stupid person.
Informants mentioned that cats can sometimes be seen chewing on wet, soapy dishrags.

connaître ses oignons *(to know one's onions)*
To be very knowledgeable, particularly in one's business or specialty.

cul plat *(flat ass)*
A foolish person.

dinde (n.m.) *(turkey)*
Fool; imbecile [Parr 1940].

emplâtre *(plaster)*
Awkward; stupid.

estragot
Silly; stupid [Parr 1940].
This term is most probably a variant of **ostrogoth**, which in France and some areas of Louisiana figuratively describes an oafish, ignorant person. The name originally described one of the Germanic (Goth) tribes living in the eastern (ost) part of their territory in Europe.
Variant: **astrogo**

être dans le panneau {à quelqu'un} *(to be in {someone's} trap)*
"To be wise to someone's tricks" [Granier 1939].
According to Duneton 1990, the term **panneau** refers to a type of small animal trap and dates back to 17th century France, where the expressions **donner dans le panneau** *(to give in the trap)* and **tomber dans le panneau** *(to fall in the trap)* both meant "to be trapped or duped by a trick."

pas bien développé *(not well developed)*
(1) Not very intelligent.
(2) Mentally retarded.

pointu *(pointed)*
Smart; intellectually astute [PNA].

posté *(posted)*
Well-informed [Parr 1940].

smatte comme une tomate *(as smart as a tomato)*
Very intelligent.
Other than the rhyming effect between the two words here, it is hard to imagine why tomatoes would be associated with intelligence. Indeed, this expression is also used ironically, particularly when embellished with other modifiers. An unintelligent person might also be: **smatte comme une tomate plate** *(as smart as a flat tomato)*
> **smatte comme une tomate fendue en quatre** *(as smart as a tomato cut in four)*
> **smatte comme tomate qui bouille dans l'eau chaude** *(as smart as a tomato boiling in hot water)*
> **smatte comme la tomate à Firin du Marais Plate** *(as smart as the tomato of Firin from Flat Swamp)*

smatte comme une fève plate *(as smart as a butter bean)*
Intelligent; or used ironically, not very intelligent.

sot comme un panier percé *(as dumb as a basket with a hole in it)*
Very stupid [Saucier 1956].

Les numéros et les marginaux

Unusual and Marginal Characters

Rightly or wrongly, societies, particularly small and homogeneous communities, have always sanctioned those who do not conform to their norms. At its most severe, such sanction has included ostracism, imprisonment and death. Fortunately, gossip and humor provide a milder outlet for our disapproval of those who are "different." The colorful repertoire of expressions used to describe marginal characters attests to their ability to pique our imaginations.

Chapitre 13

NOTE: The expressions herein are not meant to offend members of any particular ethnic group or personal persuasion, but rather to reflect the reality of the language as used in the Louisiana context, both past and present. The author asks your tolerance of the intolerant in the interest of language study.

abricot (apricot)
(1) "A queer, peculiar fellow" [Dugas 1935, Viator 1935].
(2) Something or someone unimportant.
I was unable to verify this expression in contemporary usage.
Variant: **abricotier (apricot tree).**

apostrophe (n.m./f.) (apostrophe)
A derogatory term applied to a person; "misfit," "insignificant person;" "wet blanket" [Trahan 1936, Voohries 1949, Hurst 1938, Dugas 1935].

argot (n.m.) (slang)
Derisive term applied to a person [Jeansonne 1938].

assommoir (club)
One who bores or tires others with tedious conversation [Daigle 1934].
The verb **assommer** means literally "to beat senseless," usually with a club. Its figurative meaning "to bore" is still common in France.

attrape-mouches (n.f.) (fly trap)
(1) Idiotic person (said of one who leaves mouth open) [PNA].
(2) Large mouth (said of one who talks too much) [Parr 1940].

avoir des grands doigts (to have big fingers)
To be prone to stealing [FBL].

avoir les talons jaunes (to have yellow heels)
To be old and unmarried; to be an "old maid" or "old bachelor."

avoir un ravet dans la poche (to have a roach in one's pocket)
Of a white person, to have a black ancestry [Reinecke 1971].
Most of Reinecke's expressions are from New Orleans area French. Cajuns would typically say **ravert** instead of **ravet.** This expression would be considered racist today.

bûche (n.f.) (a log)
A stupid, heavy, dull person [Pirkle 1935].

candi barré (n.m.) *(a candy cane)*
Flamboyant person; dandy [JRG].

cape-cape *(bittern or "sungazer")*
(1) An ignorant or uneducated person.
(2) A nervous person.

cataplâme (n.m.) *(a mustard plaster)*
(1) A pest; a person who hangs around unwelcome.
(2) A very awkward and slow-moving person.
Variant: **cataplasme,** usually pronounced **cataplasse.**

chatte (n.f.) *(female cat)*
"Highly sexed girl" [Jeansonne 1938].

cheval habillé en zinc *(a horse dressed in tin)*
An ill-mannered person [Calais 1968].

un [beau] coco *(a [beautiful] egg)*
An unusual character [PNA].
This is often heard in remarks such as **Ca c'est un beau coco!**, meaning *"That one's a character!"* or **Tu parles d'un beau coco, celui-là!**, meaning *"Talk about a character, that one!"*

corbeau *(crow)*
A black man.
Derogatory. Use of this term would be considered highly racist today.

cou-rouge *(red neck)*
"Those who speak English only (Yankee)"[Jeansonne 1938].

crapaud *(toad)*
(1) Short, stumpy man.
(2) "Smart aleck" [Parr 1940].

crasse (n.f.) *(scum)*
Lowly person; rascal; "low life" [Granier 1939].
This term is often used in the partitive, as in **"Ça c'est de la crasse! *(That person is some scum.)*"**

cul [de] bonbon *(candy ass)*
A dandy [PVD].
See also **candi barré**.

drigaille (n.f.) *(trash)*
"Person of low class" [Granier 1939].

embêter (v.t.)
To seduce (a young woman) or make her pregnant [PNA].

enfant inconnu *(unknown child)*
Illegitimate child [Hickman 1940].

femme placée *(placed woman)*
A woman who lives with a man, though not married to him [Parr 1940].

galérer les bancs *(to plane the benches)*
To be a wall flower at a dance [Parr 1940].

gommeux *(gummy)*
(1) Awkward, clumsy.
(2) Lazy.
(3) Dirty.

gueule rouge *(red face, literally "red muzzle")*
(1) Yankee; person from the North [DeBlanc 1935].
(2) One who speaks English but not French [Calais 1968].
In LF, the first consonant sound in **gueule** is usually pronounced like the "j" sound
in "judge."

homme clair *(clear man)*
Man not able to produce offspring; sterile man [Guilbeau 1950].

homme de paille [et pistolet de bois gras] *(a straw man [and a
wooden pistol])*
(1) Man who is a bluff [Buchanan 1931].
(2) An effeminate man [Soileau 1975].
Pistolet de bois [gras] used alone can also refer to a bluffer. Note that a **pistolet**
used without any other modifiers designates an interesting character and is not
necessarily derogatory.

macriau (n.m.) *(mackerel)*
"Man who lives with another man's wife." [Parr 1940].
The spelling is the informant's, and appears to be a phonetic rendering of the local
pronunciation of **maquerau (mackerel),** which in IF metaphorically means "pimp."

mal blanchi *(badly bleached)*
Having black ancestry, said of a white person [Reinecke 1971].
Derogatory. Use of this term would be considered racist today.

faire Pâques avant Carême *(to observe Easter before Lent)*
To become pregnant before getting married.
The metaphor plays both on the impropriety of order (Lent precedes Easter) and of celebrating (enjoying sex) before doing penitence and prayer (the marriage ceremony). Rey-Chantreau 1979 cites an old French expression in the same thematic vein to refer to having sexual relations before marriage: **faire Quasimodo avant Pâques** *(to observe Quasimodo before Easter)*. The first Sunday after Easter was traditionally known as *Quasimodo*, the name taken from the Latin words which began the liturgy of that day. Another French expression **la grange est pleine avant la moisson** *(the barn is full before the harvest)*, dating from the 17th century, is used to convey the same metaphorical idea [Duneton 1990]. In western France, the equivalent expression is **fêter Pâques avant les Rameaux** *(to celebrate Easter before Palm Sunday)* [Rézeau 1984].

oeuf de caïman *(alligator egg)*
Illegitimate child [Hurst 1938].

oeuf de carencro *(vulture egg)*
Illegitimate child [TBN].

pistolet *(a pistol)*
An unusual and interesting character, often with a dynamic personality.
Variant: **pistolet à deux manches** *(a two-handled pistol)* [Viator 1935].

popotte (n.f.)
Harlot [Hurst 1938].

pote (n.m.) *(friend IF)*
"Woman chaser" [Calais 1968].

poulet d'herbe *(grass chicken)*
An illegitimate child.
Informant PD explains that chickens sometimes lay eggs in the field instead of "at home" in the coop.

rabougri *(a stubby plant, a "runt")*
"An ungainly person" [Trahan 1936].

rester pour graine *(to stay for seed; to "go to seed")*
To remain an old maid; to not marry in one's lifetime.

somnambule (n.f.) *(sleepwalker IF)*
A fortune-teller [Dugas 1935].

suce-fleurs *(a hummingbird)*
Effeminate male [KAG].

suceur (n.m.) *(sucker)*
Homosexual [Calais 1968].

tirer la bonne aventure {à quelqu'un} *(to throw the good adventure {to someone})*
To tell one's fortune [CCC]

vénus *(Venus)*
A woman of mixed Caucasian and American Indian descent [Daigle 1934].

veuve rabiotte (n.f.) *(surplus widow)*
A woman whose husband has left her [DeBlanc 1935].

Les forts et les resistants
The Strong and the Resilient

From the earliest colonization efforts in Louisiana, tales of hardship and battles against adversity–heat, disease, storms and floods–have been part of the story. The dramatic odyssey of the Acadian people is no exception. This chapter pays homage to those who prevailed over their trials and tribulations.

Chapitre 14

s'amarrer le coeur *(to tie fast one's heart)*
To be brave; to brace oneself [Faulk 1977].

avoir la peau dure comme un cocodrie *(to have a hard skin like an alligator)*
To be a tough person [PNA].

se débattre comme un diable dans un bénitier *(to struggle like a devil in a holy water font)*
(1) To fight with fury; to squirm [Buchanan 1931].
(2) To struggle to get out of a bad situation.
In Terrebonne Parish, informants used **se débattre comme le diable dans de l'eau bénie** *(to struggle like the Devil in holy water)*, and one Lafourche informant brought the image more down to earth: **débattre comme un chat dans l'eau bénie** *(to struggle like a cat in holy water)* [OT]. See also **grenouille de bénitier**.

dégréer Saint Pierre pour gréer Saint Paul *(to unrig St. Peter in order to rig up St. Paul)*
To "rob Peter in order to pay Paul;" to take something from a place where it is needed in order to use it somewhere else; to use one's funds reserved for one thing to pay for another.
According to *The Facts on File Encyclopedia of Word and Phrase Origins*, both the English and French versions of this locution date back to at least the 14th century, and possibly derive from a 12th century Latin expression referring the the Apostles: "As it were that one would crucify Paul in order to redeem Peter." As in the English version, one LF variant makes no reference to the saints at all: **dégréer Pierre pour agréer Paul** *(to unrig Peter to rig up Paul)* [LO]. According to Parr 1940, the variant **dégréer Saint Paul pour gréer Saint Pierre** means *"to take a button from one dress to put on another."*

faire de ses pieds et ses mains pour arriver *(to use one's feet and hands to accomplish something)*
[Saucier 1956].
The source did not document the metaphorical meaning of this expression, but it would appear to mean "to make great efforts to do something."

faire des démarches *(to take steps)*
To go out of one's way; to make an extra effort [BB].

faire diable et son train *(to act like the devil and his noise)*
To make much effort [Calais 1968].

fait du nerf et de la babiche *(made of nerve and rawhide)*
Resilient, in speaking of a person; able to withstand adversity
and hardship.
The sense of **babiche** as "rawhide" is also known in Canada. According to *Le Trésor de la langue française*, its origins are in the Micmac word **ababich**, meaning "cord" or "rope."

manger les grillots avec le tactac *(to eat the unpopped seeds along with the popcorn)*
To take the good with the bad; to make the best of a situation.
CV of Beaumont shared this expression with me, explaining that he heard it from his cousin in Vermilion Parish. I have not been able to verify it as being used anywhere else, but people I mentioned it to immediately were able to guess its meaning. The spelling of **grillot** is problematic, since I could find no closely similar IF word from which it seems to be derived. The spelling **grelot**, as cited in Daigle 1984, would render a pronunciation "greulo," but I took the liberty of inventing here a spelling which would be correctly read "greeyo," as all of the informants pronounced it.

quand on a pas de cheval on monte mulet *(when one doesn't have a horse one rides a mule)*
One has to make do with what one has [Calais 1968].

tirer le diable par la queue *(to pull the devil by the tail)*
(1) To make great efforts [Daigle 1934].
(2) To be in an embarrassed position [Daigle 1934].
(3) To be in a miserable situation; to be suffering [Saucier 1956].
(4) To fight with fury [TBN].
The expression is well-known in France.

un [vrai] diable dans un bénitier *(a [real] devil in a holy water font)*
"Said of a child who struggles or fights, especially in a sedate environment" [Reinecke 1971].
See also **se débattre comme un diable dans un bénitier.**

Les sentiments et les humeurs

Feelings and Moods

Just as the ancients thought our emotional humors were housed in various organs of the body, much of the language we use today to describe psychological states still relies on images connected to the rest of our physical selves.

Chapitre 15

amiauler (v.t.) *(to meow)*
To talk to in a soothing way; to calm.

attraper une touche *(to catch a touch)*
To get tired out, worn out [Granier 1939].
Variant: **se donner une touche** *(to give oneself a touch)*

avaler la langue *(to swallow one's tongue)*
To refuse to talk [PNA].
Variant pronunciation: **envaler la langue**.
Variant: **avaler sa langue** *(to swallow one's tongue)*

avoir froid aux yeux *(to be cold in the eyes)*
To be afraid [Saucier 1956].

avoir l'oeil sec *(to have the dry eye)*
(1) To be on the lookout [RR].
(2) To be unable to sleep.

avoir la cache *(to have the hiding place)*
To be in great fear [Hickman 1940].
Variant: **avoir une cache** [Calais 1968, Voorhies 1949]

avoir le coeur gros *(to have the big heart)*
(1) To be sad.
(2) To be about to cry.
Variant: **avoir gros coeur**

avoir le crin raide *(to have back hairs standing on end)*
To be very angry [PNA].

avoir le cul rouge *(to have the red ass)*
(1) To be angry.
(2) To have the blues [Calais 1968].

avoir le "flag" en l'air *(to have the flag in the air)*
To be eager; ready to go [PNA].

avoir le jabot de travers *(to have one's bosom sideways)*
To be in a contrary mood [Viator 1935].

avoir le vent debout *(to have the wind standing)*
(1) To be worried [Daigle 1934].
(2) To be in despair [Daigle 1934].

avoir le ventre plein {de quelque chose} *(to have a bellyful {of something})*
To be fed up with something.

avoir les narines effleurées *(to have flaring nostrils)*
To be angry.

avoir les narines ouvertes *(to have open nostrils)*
To be angry [HD].

avoir les yeux égarés *(to have "wild eyes")*
To be lost or disoriented.

avoir les zinzins
To have the blues [Hurst 1938].

avoir peur à mort *(to be afraid to death)*
To be very frightened.

avoir {quelque chose} sus le coeur *(to have {something} on one's heart)*
To be chagrined by something; to have something bothering one.

avoir un à peu près *(to have a "just about")*
To have a feeling, notion, idea [PNA].
See also **avoir pas plus d'à peu près qu'une truie aux socos.**

avoir un coeur lourd *(to have a heavy heart)*
(1) To be on the verge of tears.
(2) To be sad.

avoir un grain *(to have a grain/seed)*
To be in a contrary mood [Viator 1935].
The related expression **garder un grain {contre quelqu'un} *(to keep grain {against someone})*** *means "to hold a grudge" against someone.*

avoir un pet accroché *(to have a fart hooked on)*
(1) To be bothered by something.
(2) To be in a bad mood.
(3) To not feel well.

avoir un pet en long *(to have a sideways fart)*
(1) To be contrary, hard to get along with.
(2) To be in a cranky mood [HD].
Variants: **avoir un pet en travers** *(to have a sideways fart)*
        avoir un pet de travers *(to have a sideways fart)*

avoir un tour de lune *(to have a moon spell)*
To be in a contrary mood [Viator 1935].
Variant: **avoir un coup de lune** *(to have a moon stroke)*

avoir un tracas {pour faire quelque chose} *(to have a "bother" {to do something})*
To be obsessed with {doing something}.

avoir une boule sus le coeur *(to have a ball on the heart)*
To be heartbroken in love.

avoir une crotte d'accrochée *(to have a turd hanging on)*
To be in a bad mood.
Variant: **avoir une crotte accrochée.**

avoir une dent contre {quelqu'un} *(to have a tooth against {someone})*
To hold something against someone [Saucier 1956].

avoir une indigestion de {quelque chose/quelqu'un}
To be fed up with {something/someone} [Calais 1968].

avoir une mine de chien *(to have a "dog look")*
(1) To look depressed, to look sad.
(2) To look badly groomed [Reinecke 1971].
(3) To look ill [Reinecke 1971].

avoir une tête de poule *(to have a hen's head)*
To have a poor memory [Saucier 1956].

babine (n.f.) *(lower lip)*
Pouting expression.
This term is most frequently heard in expressions such as **faire une babine** *(to make a lower lip)*, **faire des babines** *(to make lower lips)* or **pendre la babine** *(to hang the lower lip)*, which all mean "to pout." PNA also gives "to be sad or depressed" as a definition. See also **faire un gombo de babine.**
Variant: **faire la baboune** [Guilbeau 1950].

bouillonner (v.i.) *(to boil)*
To be very angry [Dugas 1935].

se braquer sur *(to aim at or to focus on)*
To be obsessed by.

changer son fusil d'épaule *(to change one's rifle to the other shoulder)*
To change one's opinion [Simon 1991].

ça fait bouillir sa chaudière *(that boils his/her pot)*
That makes him/her angry [Brandon 1955].

choqué au fiel *(to be angry to the gall bladder)*
Very angry.

cogner {quelqu'un} comme une bol de merde *(to hit {someone} like a bowl of shit)*
To become suddenly apparent to someone, usually said of an important idea or realization.
Note that **bol** is typically feminine in LF.

être dans les nués *(to be in the clouds)*
(1) To be very happy [PNA].
(2) To be in a dream world [PF].

être dans sa sauce *(to be in one's sauce)*
To be doing what one likes to do [PNA].

être dans son plat *(to be in one's plate)*
To be doing what one really wants to do [PNA].

être de travers *(to be sideways, askew)*
To be in a bad mood.
Variant: **être en travers.**

être dans son sirop *(to be in one's syrup)*
To relish one's own situation [Reinecke 1971].

être piment contre quelqu'un *(to be pepper against someone)*
To be angry with someone [Brandon 1955].

s'étouffer de rire *(to smother oneself laughing)*
To laugh excessively [Granier 1939].

être sur les épingles *(to be on the pins)*
To be excited [OV].

fâché comme un chien enragé *(as angry as a rabid dog)*
Very angry.

fâché comme un taureau *(as angry as a bull)*
Very angry.

fâché comme un tigre *(as angry as a tiger)*
Very angry.

fâché comme une dinde *(as angry as a turkey)*
Very angry [BBF].

fâché comme une garce *(as angry as a witch)*
Very angry [PNA].

fâché comme une guêpe *(as angry as a wasp)*
Very angry.

fâché comme une hornette *(as angry as a hornet)*
Very angry [RB].

faire du mauvais sang {à quelqu'un} *(to make bad blood {to someone})*
To get angry.
Variant: **se faire du mauvais sang** *(to make oneself some bad blood)* [Calais 1968].

faire le grand/la grande *(to act big)*
To act as if one is more important than one really is; to behave arrogantly.

faire le grand pour ses culottes *(to act big for one's britches)*
To behave arrogantly [Brandon 1955].
Variant: **être trop grand pour ses culottes** *(to be too big for one's britches)*.

faire le poulain *(to act the colt)*
To be angry [Brandon 1955].

faire manger de la vache enragée {à quelqu'un} (to make {someone} eat rabid cow)
To make someone angry [JRG].

faire manger du chien enragé {à quelqu'un} (to make {someone eat} rabid dog)
To make someone angry.

faire son boudin (to make one's blood sausage)
To pout.
The image alluded to here is the sausage-like appearance of the lower lip when one pouts. Further, the word **boudin** recalls the verb **bouder (to pout)**. See also **babine.**

faire un gombo de babines (to make a gumbo of lower lips)
To sulk, usually in commiseration with others, particularly after a political loss; "to have a pity party."
In France, a similar motif, **manger de la soupe à la grimace (to eat grimace soup)** describes what a husband endures when his wife is angry with him. See also: **babine.**

se fendre la gueule à rire (to split one's muzzle laughing)
To laugh heartily.
In LF, the first consonant sound in **gueule** is usually pronounced like the "j" sound in "judge." It is sometimes spelled **dgeule**.

flamber les yeux (to flame the eyes)
To stare with curiosity [Olivier 1937].

foutre le feu {à quelqu'un} (to throw the fire {on someone})
To anger {someone} [MM].

frais/fraîche comme un lapin (as fresh as a rabbit)
Invigorated; ready to go; fiesty; energetic.

se gourmer (to put on the curb chain)
(1) To get puffed up with anger.
(2) To pout [PVD].
La gourmette is the short length of chain in a horse's bridle which fastens on either side of the bit and is worn underneath the chin as an added means of controlling the animal. In France, **se gourmer** means metaphorically "to affect a stiff demeanor," as the appearance of a tightly reined horse whose neck is arched and nose is pointed down. Both definitions above are related to the image of the reined horse in that they describe controlled anger, before the point of the outburst.

je suis pas plus chien que boule (n.m.) *(I'm not any more dog than bulldog)*

I am as good as anyone else.

This reply is usually given in response to a putdown. **Boule** is an abbreviated form of **bouledogue**, which was borrowed from the English "bulldog" during the 18th century.

se lever sur le mauvais pied *(to get up on the wrong foot)*

(1) To be in a bad mood [PNA].

(2) To start things off badly [Saucier 1956].

se manger de rage *(to eat oneself up with rage)*

To be very angry; to be enraged [FBL].

mettre de l'eau dans son vin *(to put water in one's wine)*

To calm down; to temper one's remarks, particularly when angry.

mettre sa bouche en papillotes *(to put one's mouth in sparkles IF)*

To put on airs [Soileau 1975].

Daigle's *Dictionary of the Cajun Language* gives only "hair curler" for **papillote**. In IF, the term can refer to paper hair curlers, but its original IF meaning, "glitter" or "sparkle" seems to better explain the origin of this expression. According the *Le Nouveau Petit Robert I*, in Old French, **papillot** was a diminutive form of **papillon (butterfly)**, which no doubt suggested the iridescence of butterflies' wings.

monter sur ses grands chevaux *(to mount one's big horses)*

To behave arrogantly or self-righteously; to "get on one's high horse" [PNA].

pétard *(firecracker)*

Person with a dynamic or eccentric personality; a "character."

pétarade *(rapid series of explosions)*

Proud person [Daigle 1934].

Variant: **pétarde (n.f.)** [Hurst 1938].

péteux *(farter)*

(1) An arrogant person; "a smart aleck" [KAG].

(2) A shiftless person [PNA].

un petit chien [de ma chienne] *(a puppy [from my dog])*

Delayed vengence; rancor.

Used in expressions such as **je soigne un petit chien pour lui** *(I'm taking care of a* *little dog for him)*, j'ai un petit [chien] de ma chienne pour lui *(I have a little puppy from my dog for him),* it always conveys the idea that the speaker holds a grudge or is waiting for an opportune moment to obtain revenge. See also **soigner un petit veau** below.

un petit coup de grandeur *(a little stroke of greatness)*
Something done as a show off act [Simon 1991].

un petit couteau *(a little knife)*
Someone who's worthless, usually who thinks a lot of himself [PF].

soigner un petit veau {pour quelqu'un} *(to care for a little calf {for someone})*
To await or plan a moment of revenge against someone [PF].
See also **un petit chien de ma chienne** above .

rire à se foutre par terre *(to laugh to the point of throwing oneself on the ground)*
To laugh very heartily.
Variant: **rire à se péter par terre *(to laugh to the point of throwing oneself on the ground)***.

une sainte mitouche *(a holy "touch-me-not")*
(1) One who is aloof [Dugas 1935, Jeansonne 1938, Trahan 1936].
(2) A hypocrite; one who pretends to be innocent [Guilbeau 1950, Coco 1933].
Variant for (2): **une sainte nitouche** [Calais 1968].

s'il croit avoir fait l'oeuvre du Bon Dieu, qu'il espère sa bénédiction *(if he thinks he's done the work of God, may he wait for his benediction)*
Justice will prevail (repudiation of someone who thinks he's right) [MD].

son vanteur est mort *(his bragger is dead)*
He/she is a braggart [Simon 1991].
Said critically of one who feels the need to brag about himself, "since no one else will do it."

sorti de la cuisse de Jupiter *(out of Jupiter's thigh)*
"Said critically of a person or family with ancestral pretension" [Reinecke 1971].

taureau *(bull)*
(1) Someone who thinks he's better or stronger than others [EM].
(2) "A tough guy."

le taureau sur le côteau *(the bull on the hill)*
(1) The toughest or strongest of a group.
(2) The leader.
Variants: **taureau sus le côteau *(bull on the hill)***
        taureau du côteau *(bull of the hill)*

le taureau sur la butte *(the bull on the hill)*
(1) The toughest or strongest of a group.
(2) The leader [PVD].

t'es après venir trop grand pour tes culottes *(you're getting too big for your britches)*
You're being arrogant [PD].

Les menteurs et les hypocrites
Liars and Hypocrites

Louisiana politicians have a reputation for being masters at the fine art of manipulating language to suit their versions of truth, but they are certainly not the sole tellers of tales. This chapter gives examples which run the gamut from "white lie" to outright treachery.

Chapitre 16

arracheur de dents *(a tooth-puller)*
A habitual and bad liar.

Often heard in the simile **menteur comme un arracheur de dents**, it is first chronicled in 17th century France, and is known as well today in Acadian Canada and parts of France. Popular etymology says that its roots (pardon the pun) can be found in the soothing words "now this won't hurt a bit" typically associated with dental practitioners. In a modern twist, Louisianians also use **menteur comme un dentiste *(liar like a dentist)***.

catholique à gros grains *(a "big bead" catholic)*
(1) A Catholic who ignores many rules of the Church.
(2) A hypocritical Catholic who makes a show of observing liturgical rites but does not behave morally.
(3) A very fervent or fanatic Catholic.

According to Duneton 1990, this expression can be traced back to 16th century France. The **grains** in question were the beads of the rosary, so that a **catholique à gros grains** was one who in prayer would skip the smaller and more numerous beads representing the "Hail Mary" and say only the "Our Fathers." In its linguistic evolution in Louisiana, this expression has undergone several shifts in meaning.

chanter des midis à quatorze heures *(to sing noon at two p.m.)*
(1) To exaggerate; to say things which cannot be true [PF].
(2) To tell a long story; to talk on and on [Saucier 1956].

In France, a very similar expression, **chercher midi à quatorze heures *(to look for noon at two p.m.),*** is documented as early as the mid-1600s to mean "to look for something where it is not likely to be"; "to try to prolong an affair" and eventually evolves to mean "to explain something simple and clear in a long and convoluted fashion"; "to look for difficulties where there are none" [Duneton 1990]. See also: **midi à quatorze heures**.

un couteau à deux taillants *(a double-edged knife)*
A hypocrite; a two-faced flatterer.

croche comme un baril de serpents *(crooked as a barrel of snakes)*
Very crooked; very corrupt.

Often used to refer to politicians, this expression can also refer to things which are physically crooked. In the fishing community of Bayou Lafourche, one also hears **croche comme un baril de hameçons *(crooked as a barrel of fishing hooks)***.
Other variants: **croche comme un serpent *(as crooked as a snake)***
　　　　　　　croche comme un baril *(as crooked as a barrel)*.

déchirer le gingas [en travers] *(to tear the gingham crosswise)*
To tell a falsehood.
Although it appears to refer literally to tearing a fabric on the bias, the origin of this expression is obscure. (**Gingas** also refers literally in LF to a Black and White Rock Island chicken.). Interestingly, Rey and Chantreau 1979 cite the IF **de guingois,** an expression which is attested as early as the 1400s, and which in itself means "crosswise." The term seems to derive from the old verb **guiger** or **guinger,** which became **ginguer (to jump around).** The connection is unclear but worth exploring.

embeurrer *(to butter)*
To flatter for the purpose of one's own gain; to "butter up."

faire des contes *(to tell tales)*
To lie.

faire le filou comme un chien basset *(to act the sly one like a basset hound)*
To do things while trying not to be noticed; to have a guilty look on one's face [ABR].

filou comme un renard *(sly as a fox)*
Very sly [Brandon 1955].

jouer bibi la pelote {avec quelqu'un} *(to play "bibi la pelote" with {someone})*
To avoid telling the truth to someone; to give someone "the runaround".
Bibi la pelote was a popular children's game in the 1930s and 40s. It was a sort of primitive form of golf combined with dodgeball, played with sticks, balls and cans.
Variant: **jouer à la pelote {avec quelqu'un}** *(to play ball {with someone}).*

jouer la patte de cochon *(to play the pig's foot)*
To play a dirty trick [Saucier 1956].

licher (v.t.) *(to lick)*
To flatter for the purpose of one's own gain; to "butter up" [Dugas 1935].

macorner (v.t.) *(to yoke)*
To fool or trick {someone} [PNA].
See also **se macorner avec.**

mentir comme un dentiste *(to lie like a dentist)*
To lie a lot.
See also: **arracheur de dents.**

micmac
Foul play; intrigue; dishonesty [Parr 1940].

monstre (n.f.) *(monster)*
Scoundrel; rascal [Parr 1940].

originel *(original)*
Scoundrel; rascal [Jeansonne 1938].

un pain de sucre *(a sweet bread)*
(1) A hypocrite who appears very virtuous to others.
(2) A person with stiff manners [Bernard 1933].

par en dessous *(underneath)*
Sneaky.

passer comme un éclair *(to pass like a lightning bolt)*
(1) To be easily accepted as true (of a falsehood) [PF].
(2) To happen quickly [PNA].

passer des crêpes {à quelqu'un} *(to pass {someone} some pancakes)*
To trick; to "pull a fast one" on someone [TBB].

passer une bleue {à quelqu'un} *(to pass someone a "blue")*
To tell a fib to someone.
Une belle bleue *(a beautiful blue)* is a big lie [BGM].

sauter crapaud {pour quelqu'un} *(to "leap frog" {for someone})*
To be a "yes man" for someone; to slavishly obey or follow.
This expression usually refers to blind or fawning loyalty to a boss or political patron.

tirer une carotte *(to pull up a carrot)*
To tell a falsehood [Daigle 1934].

traître comme la mort *(as treacherous as death)*
A terrible traitor [Saucier 1956].

tu peux pas me beurrer avec ça *(You can't butter me with that)*
You can't fool me with that [HD].

tu peux pas me sucrer avec ça *(You can't sugar me with that)*
You can't fool me with that [HD].

Les vaut-rien et les criminels

The Worthless and the Crooks

At their best, they are only annoying or exasperating, but at least we can count on them to make the rest of us look good. They can be co-workers, neighbors and in-laws, sometimes even our children or spouses. At their worst, they inspire fear and loathing. We read about them in the paper and wonder about the nature of evil. These are the folks whose most remarkable characteristics are exaggerations of those traits we like least in ourselves.

Chapitre 17

The lazy, the whiners, and the worthless:

attraper un coup de lilas *(to get a chinaball tree-stroke)*
To be afflicted with laziness; to be lazy.
I was never able to verify this expression with anyone other than PVD, but its originality makes it worth including. The irony comes from the juxtaposition of a **coup de soleil (sunstroke)** and a **lilas parasol (chinaball tree)**, a tree known for its generous summer shade. One afflicted with such an imaginary malady is typically lazy because he's been resting in the shade all day.

avoir larme près de l'oeil *(to have a tear near the eye)*
To have a tendency to whine or cry easily.
In a more potent version, it is said of a whiner/complainer, **il a larme à l'oeil et la crotte au cul** *(he has a tear in the eye and a turd in the ass)*.

ça craque pas fort *(that doesn't crack very loudly)*
That is of little value [GDC].
The pronoun **ça** can also mean "they" (of people) in LF.

caca pour merde *(caca for shit)*
(1) One is as bad as the other [Lanclos 1992].
(2) It's over and done with [TBB].

casser le petit bâton *(to break the little stick)*
To break a promise not to indulge in something [Lanclos 1992].

chiquer du vieux linge *(to chew on old clothes)*
To complain incessantly [Olivier 1937].

couper avec une hache à deux taillants *(to cut with a two-bladed hatchet)*
To be very critical of others; to criticize incessantly [PNA].

dépendeur d'andouilles *(one who unhooks andouille)*
"One who does not do important or stressful work" [Reinecke 1971].
Andouille is a type of sausage, so that the job of removing the final product from the hook seems laughable in comparison to the work involved in producing it. In France, however, this same expression, documented as early as 1840, describes a very tall, gangly person. French kitchens of old had high ceilings, requiring a very tall person to unhook the sausages that were hung there to cure [Duneton 1990].

le jeu [en] vaut pas la chandelle *(the game is not worth the candle)*
It's not worth the trouble or risk.
Informants in Terrebonne Parish explain that the "candle" in question was the one burned during a card game for which the betting stakes were not high enough to offset the cost of the lighting. This expression is still used in IF also.

pas casser la rate *(to not rupture the spleen)*
To not work; to be lazy in one's work [PNA].

passer son temps à couper les cheveux en quatre *(to spend one's time cutting hairs in four)*
"To find fault where there is little or no cause" [Saucier 1956].
The image of cutting or "splitting" hairs as used to describe a person's inordinate obsession with details is well known in English and French, and indeed, **couper les cheveux en quatre** *(to cut hairs in four)* in France means to be a stickler for details, though not necessarily in the context of a complaint.

un pet dans un ouragan *(a fart in a hurricane)*
Something of little consequence or importance.
Variant: **ça compte pas plus qu'un pet dans un ouragan** *(that doesn't count any more than a fart in a hurricane)*.

le postier à Paris va jamais voir ça *(the postman in Paris will never say that)*
That's an error of no importance; don't worry about it [EC].
This is usually said to comfort the person who has made the error. The variant form **Reagan va jamais voir ça** shows a vitality in Louisiana French in its ability to adapt to contemporary situations.

pot fêlé *(cracked pot)*
Someone who is frequently complaining that something is wrong with his or her health [Soileau 1975].

pratique (n.f.) à chagrin *(a practice of unhappiness)*
Said of a person who constantly complains and whines [Soileau 1975].

traîner les savates *(to drag one's slippers)*
"To lag behind in one's work" [Viator 1935].

The following expressions are used to speak of things or people which are considered to be worthless or of very little value.

ça compte pas plus qu'un pet dans la poussière *(that doesn't count any more than a fart in the dust)*
That is of little value [MV].

The pronoun **ça** can also refer to people.

ça vaut pas baisser et ramasser *(that's not worth leaning over to pick up)*
That is worthless; it has little or no redeeming value [WDD].

The pronoun **ça** can also mean "they" (of people) in LF.

ça vaut pas Caillette et son veau *(that's not worth Caillette and her calf)*
That is worthless; it has little or no redeeming value [BB].

The pronoun **ça** can also mean "they" (of people) in LF.

ça vaut pas cinq sous de pistaches *(that's not worth five cents' worth of peanuts)*
That is worthless; it has little or no redeeming value [WDD].

The pronoun **ça** can also mean "they" (of people) in LF.

ça vaut pas la balle pour le tuer *(that's not worth the bullet to kill it with)*
That is worthless; it has little or no redeeming value [PNA].

The pronoun **ça** can also mean "they" (of people) in LF.

ça vaut pas la cartouche [pour le tirer avec] *(that's not worth the cartridge [to shoot it with])*
That is worthless; it has little or no redeeming value.

The pronoun **ça** can also mean "they" (of people) in LF.

ça vaut pas merde *(that's not worth shit)*
That is worthless; it has little or no redeeming value.

The pronoun **ça** can also mean "they" (of people) in LF.

Variants: **ça vaut pas la merde**
   ça vaut pas une merde.

ça vaut pas la poudre pour l'essouffler au diable *(that's not worth the gunpowder to blow it to the devil)*
That is worthless; it has little or no redeeming value [OT].

The pronoun **ça** can also mean "they" (of people) in LF.

ça vaut pas le lapin du curé *(that's not worth the pastor's rabbit)*
That is worthless; it has little or no redeeming value [Saucier 1956].
The pronoun **ça** *can also mean "they" (of people) in LF.*

ça vaut pas les quatre fers d'un cheval mort *(that's not worth the four horseshoes on a dead horse)*
That is worthless; it has little or no redeeming value [Buchanan 1931].
The pronoun **ça** *can also mean "they" (of people) in LF.*

ça vaut pas les quatre fers d'un chien *(that's not worth the four horseshoes on a dog)*
That is worthless; it has little or no redeeming value [Calais 1968].
The pronoun **ça** *can also mean "they" (of people) in LF.*

ça vaut pas les quatre pattes d'un chien *(that's not worth the four paws of a dog)*
That is worthless; it has little or no redeeming value.
The pronoun **ça** *can also mean "they" (of people) in LF.*

ça vaut pas les quatre pattes d'un chien crêvé *(that's not worth the four paws of a dead dog)*
That is worthless; it has little or no redeeming value [FP].
The pronoun **ça** *can also mean "they" (of people) in LF.*

ça vaut pas les quatre pattes d'un chien maigre *(that's not worth the four paws of a skinny dog)*
That is worthless; it has little or no redeeming value [RJG].
The pronoun **ça** *can also mean "they" (of people) in LF.*

ça vaut pas tuer à coups de bâton *(that's not worth killing with blows from a stick)*
That is worthless; it has little or no redeeming value [PVD].
The pronoun **ça** *can also mean "they" (of people) in LF.*

ça vaut pas un pet *(that's not worth a fart)*
That is worthless; it has little or no redeeming value [Hurst 1938].
The pronoun **ça** *can also mean "they" (of people) in LF.*

ça vaut pas un pétard *(that's not worth a firecracker)*
That is worthless; it has little or no redeeming value.
The pronoun **ça** *can also mean "they" (of people) in LF.*

ça vaut pas une chique *(that's not worth a chaw)*
That is worthless; it has little or no redeeming value.
The pronoun **ça** can also mean "they" (of people) in LF.

ça vaut pas une pistache *(that's not worth a peanut)*
That is worthless; it has little or no redeeming value [PVD].
The pronoun **ça** can also mean "they" (of people) in LF.

pas assez bon pour faire du savon *(not good enough to make soap with)*
Worthless.
This expression appears to allude to the practice of sending old, worn-out animals such as horses to "the soap factory" once their usefulness wears out.

Taupin vaut Maurin *(Taupin is worth Maurin)*
(1) Of two things or people, one is as good/bad as the other.
(2) There is no point in arguing [Reinecke 1971].
In IF, the expressions **taupin vaut marotte** and **taupin vaut taupine** are used to describe two equally ugly or bad people. The *Dictionary of the Cajun Language* describes a **taupin** as a "burly man." According to *Le Nouveau Petit Robert I*, the term comes from **taupe** *(mole)* and originally referred to soldiers who planted land mines. **Marotte** originally referred to a buffoon's scepter, and later to a caprice or favorite hobby. With its significance lost somewhere along the way in Louisiana, **marotte** appears to have evolved into the common family name **Maurin**, and **Taupin** also becomes a person's name, perhaps in the interest of symmetry.

l'un vaut l'autre et l'autre vaut rien *(one is worth the other and the other is worth nothing)*
Of two things or people, neither is worth much.
Variant: **l'un vaut l'autre et les deux vaut (valent) rien** *(one is worth the other and the two are worth nothing)* [Coco 1933].

The hateful and the criminal:

avoir la langue comme une vipère *(to have a tongue like a viper)*
To be caustic in one's speech [PF].

bourreau (n.m.) *(executioner)*
(1) A mean, grouchy person.
(2) A bully.

coeur noir *(black heart)*
A base, despicable person.

langue de serpent *(serpent tongue)*
A malicious person who speaks badly of others.
See also: **avoir la langue de vipère** *(to have the viper's tongue)*.

mettre le grappin {sur quelqu'un} *(to put the grappling hook {on someone})*
To steal from someone [Viator 1935].

palais bleu *(blue palate)*
A very mean person.
Can be used with **avoir** *(to have)* *or* **être** *(to be)*. *Supposedly, this is a reference to the dark colored palate of some dogs.* **Palais noir** *(black palate)* *is a variant with the same meaning.*

pichou (a., n.m, n.f.) *(bobcat)*
1) Mean [Trahan 1936].
2) Mean person [Parr 1940].
3) Mean woman [DeBlanc 1935].

pichouette (n.f.)
(1) Mean woman [Granier 1939].
(2) Spry, mischievous little girl.

pirate (2) *(pirate)*
Mean, unkind person [Guilbeau 1950].

pirater {quelqu'un} *(to pirate {someone})*
To steal from someone [PNA].

ratatouille (n.f.) *(type of stew)*
(1) Contemptible people/person [Hurst 1938].
(2) A beating or spanking.
(3) A heavy rain [Daigle 1984].

ratché (a.)
Stingy; avaricious [KAG].

sac à tous grains *(all-seed sack)*
A temperamental person [Viator 1935].

sans coeur (n.m./f.) *(without heart)*
Hard, pitiless person [Granier 1939].

soulager {quelqu'un} de son porte-monnaie *(to relieve {someone} of his/her wallet)*
To steal someone's wallet [Saucier 1956].

tirer une chique {à quelqu'un} *(to throw a chaw {at someone})*
To say something mean to someone; to make a caustic remark.
Few things are more disgusting than a wad of tabacco which has been chewed and spit out, particularly if a malicious chewer has aimed in one's direction. **Un tireur de chiques** *(a chaw thrower)* or **un passeur de chiques** *(passer of chaws)* is someone who makes caustic remarks.
Variant: **passer une chique** *(to pass a chaw)*

vache habillée en zinc *(a cow dressed in tin)*
Hateful, mean person [Calais 1968].

yeux barrés *(striped eyes)*
An evil or bad person; a scoundrel.
Variants: **yeux barrés comme le diable** *(striped-eyed like the devil)*
　　　　　yeux barrés comme un cabri *(striped-eyed like a goat)* [PVD]

Les commencements et les fins

Beginnings and Endings

This chapter includes a variety of ways in which we can talk about the firsts and lasts of our lives, both the watershed moments and the everyday incidents.

adieu la calèche *(good-bye to the carriage)*
According to Voohries1949 and Calais1968, this exclamation was uttered jokingly when something fell and broke. Though I have been unable to find LF speakers who use this expression today, Duneton 1990 includes an 18th century quote describing a similar IF expression, **adieu la valise**, which means "all is lost."

avoir son baptême *(to have one's baptism)*
To do something for the first time.
Along the same theme, the verb **baptiser *(to baptise)*** can be used figuratively to speak of trying or using something for the first time.

avoir tiré son pétard *(to have thrown one's firecracker)*
To have come to the end of one's high point; to be on the decline [PNA].

baille a couru [sa course] *(the bay has run [its race])*
It's all over; it's too late now.
This is probably French Louisiana's most common expression of resignation to a situation, which is not surprising, given our love of horseracing. The word **baille *(bay colored)***, which dates back to 14th century France, is lost to most modern-day Frenchmen, though some rural speakers in France might still use the derivative **baillet** to describe a reddish-brown horse or cow.

cailler la botte *(to curdle the boot)*
To die [Viator 1935].
Possibly related to the old expression **caillebotter** meaning **to clabber, to coagulate**.

casser la pipe *(to break the pipe)*
To die [Olivier 1937].
This expression was documented in France as early as 1855 [Duneton 1990].

c'est bernique! *(it's barnacle!)*
It's all over, too bad, all is lost.
I've given the literal translation above for the word **bernique**, also spelled **bernicle**, though in Louisiana, its metaphorical usage seems to completely overshadow any other. Duneton 1990 quotes from the *Dictionnaire de Langue Verte* (1867) the entry **bernicle sansonnet!** as having essentially the same metaphorical meaning as this Cajun version. In IF, **sansonnet** is a synonym for **étourneau *(starling)***.

c'est sellé et bridé *(it's saddled and bridled)*
Said of a situation in which all is complete, nothing is missing [Daigle 1934].

cinq sous commencent la piastre *(five cents start the dollar)*
Getting started is the hardest part of a project [RH].

We have many English expressions which convey a similar message: "Rome wasn't built in a day.";"the journey of a thousand miles begin with the first step." In Quebec, the same money motif is used in an expression admonishing someone who is never quite satisfied: **il te manque toujours cinq sous pour la piastre *(you're always missing five cents to make the dollar)*** [MD].

craquer (v.i.) *(to crack)*
To die [Granier 1939].

faire la croix *(to make the sign of the cross)*
To swear not to do something again.

The implication is that the speaker has "learned his or her lesson" or been mistreated for the last time.

Variant: **faire sa croix *(to make one's sign of the cross)*.**

fumer la pipe *(to smoke the pipe)*
To die [Viator 1935].

mettre en cannelle *(to put something into cinnamon)*
To tear into pieces [Voorhies 1949].

paner la botte *(to ?? the boot)*
To die [Viator 1935].

It's not clear whether the verb in this expression is **paner *(to coat with breading for cooking)*** or **panner *(to hit with the back of a hammer)***. However, it is clear that boots have long been associated with death in IF. From 17th century France, **il y a laissé ses bottes *(he left his boots there)*** means "he died." From the 19th century, the expression **graisser ses bottes *(to grease one's boots)*** means "to receive the last sacraments; to prepare oneself to die" [Duneton 1990].

tomber en botte *(to fall into "boot")*
To fall into ruin or disrepair; to become delapidated.

DesRuisseaux 1979 suggests that the origin of this expression, which is known in France, lies in the often poor quality and lack of durability of boots of olden times. In maritime IF, the term means an intentional dismantling of certain necessary items on a ship in order to save space.

Variants: **tomber en doise** (Parr 1940)
         tomber en val et en zèle [Parr 1940].

.

Les erreurs et les échecs
Mistakes and Failures

Though we may sometimes take malicious pleasure in pointing out the failings of others, it is certainly never pleasant to admit our own mistakes or point out those of our loved ones to them. Here are some colorful, if not always delicate ways to broach the subject.

Chapitre 1 9

à la va vite *(go quickly style)*
Quickly and not very well [Lanclos 1992].

chier sa crotte de noces *(to shit one's wedding turd)*
To give a great effort to do something and not succeed [BRB].

chier sur le palonnier *(to shit on the swing bar)*
To make a big mistake; to fail in one's effort.
The"swing bar" goes behind a horse harnessed to a wagon or buggy.
Variants: **chier dessus le palonnier**
        chier sus le palonnier

dételer le wagon au milieu du marais *(to unharness the wagon in the middle of the swamp)*
To give up in the middle of an undertaking [Lanclos 1992].

dételer le mulet dans le milieu des rangs *(to unharness the mule in the middle of the rows)*
To give up in the middle of an undertaking [TBB].

faire {quelque chose} à la six-quatre-deux *(to do {something} six-four-two style)*
To do something badly, poorly, backwards; to be negligent in doing something [Soileau 1975].
According to Duneton 1990, this expression first appeared in France in the mid-nineteenth century, with essentially the same meaning as in LF.

faire {quelque chose} à tambour battant *(to do {something} to beat the drum)*
To do something quickly and not well [Lanclos 1992].

faire un pas en avant et deux en arrière *(to take one step forward and two steps backward)*
To not advance well; to be unable to get ahead despite some progress [MBG].

faire une coche mal taillée *(to make a badly carved notch)*
To make a big mistake [MV].
In France, according to Rey and Chantreau 1979, the remarkably similar 16th century expression **une côte mal taillée** means figuratively an "approximation" and more often "a compromise that satisfies no one". Originally, **une côte** was a fee or tax that was badly or unevenly distributed, though that sense is lost except in very specific fields.

Taillée in financial circles had the meaning of "separated for a share." Louisianians, though, would find this etymology obscure, since the image of the woodworker botching a cut quite clearly conveys the notion of error.

goudronner (v.t.) *(to tar up)*
To mess up [Jeansonne 1938].

lâcher la patate *(to drop the potato)*
(1) To give up.
(2) To mess up.

lâcher la baratte *(to drop the churn)*
To give up.

There was lots of hard physical work involved in churning butter, and this task was important to the household of days gone by.

Variant: **laisser aller la baratte *(to let go of the churn)***

laisser {quelqu'un} en plan
To abandon (a friend) [Saucier 1956].

pondre un oeuf *(to lay an egg)*
(1) To mess up.
(2) To say something unbelievable [PNA].

tourner en eau de boudin *(to turn into boudin water)*
(1) To become insignificant.
(2) To not come about [Lanclos 1992, Saucier 1956].

Cajun **boudin** is a type of spicy rice-and-meat dressing stuffed into sausage casing and then simmered. The liquid which then remains is thrown out, as it has little flavor or nutritional value.

vider la mer avec un baril défoncé *(to empty the sea with a broken barrel)*
To do a task which requires great effort but accomplishes nothing [Lanclos 1992].

Les comparaisons et les contrastes
Comparisons and Contrasts

These similes often spill from our lips quite spontaneously when we look to describe extremes. We anchor our language upon such clichés, a common frame of reference for structuring our view of the world. One needn't live in Louisiana to understand being "as fat as a pig" or "as small as the eye of a needle," but it certainly helps to clarify "as red as a crawfish." Then again, what is anyone to make of a problem which is "as serious as a bushel of intestines?"

Chapitre 20

aigre comme du vin *(as bitter as wine)*
Very bitter [EB].
In Louisiana, **aigre** is often pronounced **haigre**.

aigre comme du vinaigre *(as bitter as vinegar)*
Very bitter.
In Louisiana, **aigre** is often pronounced **haigre**.

aimer comme [le] cochon aime la boue *(to love as much as the pig loves mud)*
To like very much [Brandon 1955].

aimer comme cochon aime lavure *(to love as much as the pig loves slop)*
To like very much [RJG].

aimer comme cochon aime maïs *(to love as much as the pig loves corn)*
To like very much [PNA].

amer comme du fiel (bitter as gall)
Very bitter [PNA].

amoureux comme un paon (amorous as a peacock)
Womanizing; philandering [PVD].

amoureux comme une puce (amorous as a flea)
(1) Womanizing.
(2) Deeply in love [PNA].

avoir une gueule comme un vilevaquin *(to have a muzzle like a hand drill)*
To always say the wrong thing [Parr 1940].
In LF, the first consonant sound in **gueule** is usually pronounced like the "j" sound in "judge." **Vilevaquin** appears to be a variant of **vilebrequin**. It is also sometimes pronounced **virebrequin**.

blanc comme du coton *(as white as cotton)*
Very white [Brandon 1955].

blanc comme du lait *(as white as milk)*
Very white [Saucier 1956].

blanc comme la neige *(as white as snow)*
Very white [Saucier 1956].

blanc comme un champignon *(as white as a mushroom)*
Very white [Saucier 1956].

blanc comme un linge *(as white as a sheet)*
Very white [PF].

bleu comme de l'indigo *(as blue as indigo)*
Very blue [Saucier 1956].

bleu comme le ciel *(as blue as the sky)*
Very blue.

bon comme (de) l'or *(as good as gold)*
Very good.

bon comme la vie *(as good as life)*
Very good [Buchanan 1931].

bon comme son père *(as good as one's father)*
Very good (of a person) [EM].

bon comme un ange (dessus la terre) *(as good as an angel [on the Earth])*
Very good (of a person).

campé comme un as de pique *(camped like an ace of spades)*
Rooted, stuck in one spot [Viator 1935].

clair comme de l'eau trouble *(as clear as troubled water)*
Unclear.

clair comme la boue *(as clear as mud)*
Unclear [PF].

clair comme du jus de chique *(as clear as tobacco spit)*
Unclear [Brandon 1955].
Variant: **clair comme du jus de tabac** *(as clear as tobacco spit)* [PNA].

clair comme le jour *(as clear as day)*
Very clear [PNA].

clair comme un miroir *(as clear as a mirror)*
Very clear [Brandon 1955].

collé comme un sangsue *(stuck like a leech)*
(1) Refers to a guest who won't leave.
(2) Describes an acquaintance who is a pest [JRG].

comme le fil en aiguille *(like thread into a needle)*
Very well, very smoothly.

comme un papier de musique *(like sheet music)*
(1) Very well, very smoothly (adv.).
(2) Very smooth (adj.).

comme une plume *(like a feather)*
Very well, very smoothly [FP].
Example: **danser comme une plume** *(to dance like a feather)* [PVD].

courcobiller comme un cheval *(to buck like a horse)*
To twist around [RJG].

doucement comme Chrismeusse *(as slow as Christmas)*
Very slow [MBG]; very slowly.
Though used exclusively as an adverb in IF, the word **doucement** can also be an adjective in LF. It can also mean "slow to learn" or "weak in intelligence."

doucement comme la lune
Very slow; very slowly [PVD].

doucement comme la melasse dans janvier *(as slow as molasses in January)*
Very slow; very slowly [PVD].

doucement comme une crabe *(as slow as a crab)*
Very slow; very slowly [OT].

doucement comme un colimaçon *(as slow as a slug)*
Very slow; very slowly [Brandon 1955].

doucement comme une merde *(as slow as a shit)*
Very slow; very slowly [PNA].

doucement comme une tortue *(as slow as a turtle)*
Very slow; very slowly.

doux comme le miel *(as slow/sweet as honey)*
(1) Very slow [PVD].
(2) Very sweet.
(3) Very gentle.
Variants: **doux comme du miel** *(as sweet as honey)*
           doux comme du sucre *(as sweet as sugar)*

dur comme du caillou *(as hard as a pebble)*
Very hard [TBN].

dur comme du fer *(as hard as iron)*
Very hard [Brandon 1955].

dur comme la brique *(as hard as brick)*
Very hard.

dur comme la pierre *(as hard as rock)*
Very hard.

emplâtre comme du goudron *(as awkward as tar)*
Very awkward [Brandon 1955].

entêté comme un mulet *(as hardheaded as a mule)*
Very stubborn [Brandon 1955].

être comme la tortue *(to be like the turtle)*
"To carry one's belongings on one's back" [Saucier 1956].

être comme un(e) serpent à sonnette *(to be like a rattlesnake)*
To be untrustworthy [JRG].

faquin comme un paon *(as proud as a peacock)*
Very proud; vain [HP].

fier comme un paon *(as proud as a peacock)*
Very proud; vain [PNA].

fin comme de la cendre *(as fine as ash)*
Very fine.

fin comme de la soie *(as fine as silk)*
Very fine.

fin comme la peau d'un bébé *(as fine as a baby's skin)*
Very fine, smooth.

fin comme une aiguille *(as fine as a needle)*
Very thin [ER].

fort comme la mort *(as strong as death)*
Very strong [Saucier 1956].

fort comme le diable *(as strong as the devil)*
Very strong [Saucier 1956].

fort comme un boeuf *(as strong as a bull)*
Very strong [Brandon 1955].

fort comme un cheval *(as strong as a horse)*
Very strong [Brandon 1955].

fort comme un éléphant *(as strong as an elephant)*
Very strong [Brandon 1955].

fort comme un mulet *(as strong as mule)*
Very strong [Brandon 1955].

gai comme un fou *(as gay as a fool)*
Happy, in a good humor [Saucier 1956].

gourmand comme un chien *(as gluttonous as a dog)*
Very gluttonous.

gourmand comme un cochon *(as gluttonous as a pig)*
Very gluttonous [Brandon 1955].

gros comme le ciel *(as big as the sky)*
Very big.

guetter comme un chat guette une souris *(to watch the way a cat watches a mouse)*
To watch closely [MCT].

guetter comme un détectif
To watch closely [PNA].

guetter comme un carencro guette une charogne *(to watch like a buzzard watches a carcass)*
To watch closely [MM].

heureux comme des poissons dans l'eau *(as happy as a fish in water)*
Very happy.
Variant: **heureux comme les poissons dans l'eau.**

laid comme un bouki *(as ugly as a hyena)*
Very ugly [Reinecke 1971].
The word **bouki** is of African origin, and was brought to Louisiana along with the **Bouki et Lapin** folk characters who became known as Brer Fox and Brer Rabbit in other areas of the United States. Hyenas are not native to North America, and **Bouki** in French Louisiana folklore is typically depicted as a wolf-like animal, the dimwitted victim of **Lapin's** trickery. It is doubtful that the New Orleans-area Creoles who used this expression thought of the **bouki** as an actual hyena.

laid comme un coin de banquette *(as ugly as the corner of a sidewalk/boardwalk)*
Very ugly [KAG].
In the popular song **"La Valse de Holly Beach"**, one verse tells the listener that **ta petite soeur ressemble à un coin de banquette** *(your little sister looks like the corner of a sidewalk/boardwalk).*
Variant: **vilain comme un coin de banquette** *(as ugly as the corner of a sidewalk/boardwalk).*

léger comme une plume *(as light as a feather)*
Very light [HD].

léger comme une poussière *(as light as dust)*
Very light [PNA].

maigre comme un manche à balai *(as thin as a broomstick)*
Very thin [WD].

maigre comme un pique-bois *(as thin as a woodpecker)*
Very thin [RB].

maigre comme un poteau de barrière *(as thin as a fencepost)*
Very thin.

maigre comme un tasso *(as skinny as a strip of dried meat)*
Very thin [FP].

maigre comme une aigrette *(as thin as an egret)*
Very thin [BB].

maigre comme une vieille vache *(as thin as an old cow)*
Very thin [PNA].

malade comme un carencro *(as sick as a buzzard)*
Very ill [KAG].

malade comme un chien *(as sick as a dog)*
Very sick.

mauvaise comme la gale *(as bad as mange)*
Very bad.
Variant: **maudit comme une gale** [Lanclos 1992]. (Note that **maudit** in LF can mean **damned**, **wicked** or **mischievous**, depending on the region where it is used).

mauvaise comme un(e) serpent à sonnette *(as bad as a rattlesnake)*
Very mean; very bad [PNA].

mauvaise comme une guêpe *(as bad as a wasp)*
Very mean; hateful.
Variant: **méchante comme une guêpe** *(as mean as a wasp)* [Saucier 1956].

mauvaise comme une puce *(as bad as a flea)*
Very bad [TBN].

noir comme de la suit *(as black as soot)*
Very black [HD].

noir comme du charbon *(as black as coal)*
Very black [PD].

noir comme l'as de pique *(as black as the ace of spades)*
Very black [PVD].
The informant pronounced the word for "ace" as **ars**.

noir comme un fond de chaudière *(as black as the bottom of a pot)*
Very black [EC].

nu comme un ver *(as naked as a worm)*
Completely naked.
This expression was made locally famous as an integral part of the lyrics of Camey Doucet's Cajun French version of "The Streaker."

passer comme une balle *(to pass like a bullet)*
To happen quickly.

plat comme une punaise *(as flat as a stinkbug)*
Very flat [Saucier 1956].
Although the source did not give a meaning for this expression, "very flat" is the most likely .

plate comme une merde *(as flat as a shit)*
Very flat [PNA].

plate comme une planche *(as flat as a board)*
Very flat.

porter {quelque chose} comme la peau *(to wear {something} like skin)*
To wear (as clothes) every day [Viator 1935].

rire comme un fou/une folle *(to laugh like a fool)*
To laugh heartily.

rire comme un mulet qu'a envalé des ronces *(to laugh like a mule which has swallowed brambles)*
To have a silly or guilty look on one's face.

rouge comme un piment *(as red as a pepper)*
Very red [FP].
Variant: **rouge comme du piment** *(as red as pepper)* [BB].

rouge comme une bête rouge *(as red as a redbug)*
Very red.

rouge comme une betterave *(as red as a beet)*
Very red [Saucier 1956].

rouge comme une écrevisse *(as red as a crawfish)*
Very red.

rouge comme une tomate *(as red as a tomato)*
Very red.

sérieux comme une manne de tripes *(as serious as a bushel of intestines)*
Very serious [PF].

sourd comme un pot *(as deaf as a pot)*
Very deaf [Saucier 1956, Reinecke 1971].

sourd comme un pot de chambre *(as deaf as a chamber pot)*
Very deaf.

sourd comme un poteau *(as deaf as a post)*
Very deaf [Saucier 1956].

tête dure comme un bourriquet *(as hard-headed as a donkey)*
Very stubborn.

travailler comme [un] neuf *(to work like new)*
To work well; to go smoothly.

vert comme de l'herbe *(as green as grass)*
(1) Naïve [PD]
(2) Very green in color.
Variant: **vert comme des herbes** [WD].

vilain comme le diable *(as ugly as the devil)*
Very ugly [FP].

vilain comme les sept péchés mortels *(as ugly as the seven mortal sins)*
Very ugly.
Variants: **laid comme les sept péchés mortels** *(as ugly as the seven mortal sins)*
    laid comme les sept péchés capitaux *(as ugly as the seven capital sins)* [Saucier 1956].
    maudit comme un péché mortel *(damned like a mortal sin)* [PNA].
    (note that **maudit** in LF can mean **damned**, **wicked** or **mischievous**, depending on the region where it is used)
    vilain comme un péché mortel *(as ugly as a mortal sin)*
    vilain comme un péché *(as ugly as a sin)* [RS].

vilain comme un macaque *(as ugly as a monkey)*
Very ugly [Saucier 1956].

Variant: **laid comme un macaque** *(as ugly as a monkey).*

La famille et les enfants
Family and Children

The setting is characterized by relationships at their most intimate. We cannot keep up appearances forever among the people with whom we live day in and day out. Traditionally, Cajuns and Creoles value family very strongly, though what we see reflected in this chapter is less a romantic view than a practical, down-to-earth one.

Chapitre 21

bâton de vieillesse *(old age stick)*
A person who can be depended on for help in one's old age.
Typically, this might be said of a child born late in the life of a couple: **Celui-là va être mon bâton de vieillesse.** *(This one is going to be my comfort in my later years.)*
Variant: **béquille de vieillesse** *(crutch of old age)*

bon[ne] à marier *(good enough to marry)*
Handy, adept, efficient, especially with manual tasks.

cadet (m.)
The second child of a family [Viator 1935].
Note that in IF, **cadet** is the youngest child.

capotez pas la maison! *(don't turn the house over!)*
Calm down!; quiet down! (said to unruly children) [TBN].
See also **laissez un bloque en bas de la maison!**

c'est là où mon nombril est enterré (that's where my umbilical cord is buried)
That's where I was born.
This is a reference to the folk practice of burying the nub of a baby's umbilical cord, once dried and fallen, in the family yard [ABR]. Note that **où** in LF is often spelled **é-où** or **ayoù** to render the local pronunciation.

enfant du deuxième lit *(child of a second bed)*
Child of a second marriage.

faire [sa] belle *(to act beautiful)*
(Of a baby) to stand by oneself in preparation for walking.
In IF, the related **faire le beau** describes a dog trick in which the animal stands on its hind legs by itself. Perhaps both the masculine and feminine forms were at one time used to refer to babies in LF, with the masculine form being eventually lost.
Variant: **se faire belle**

la fleur de la famille *(the flower of the family)*
The prettiest daughter of the family.

la fleur de lis *(iris)*
The seventh daughter of a family [Parr 1940].

gorgoyo (f.) *(tadpole)*
A little boy [Jeansonne 1938].

jeu de chien tourne en bataille *(dog's game becomes a fight)*
Horseplay can lead to an argument.

A proverbial observation typically made while watching children play. It reminds us that friendly games and teasing often turn into real fights.

Variants: **jeu de chien finit en bataille** *(dog's game ends in fighting)*
jeu de chien, jeu de vilain *(dog's game, wicked game)*

laissez un bloque en bas de la maison! *(leave a block under the house!)*
Calm down!; quiet down! (said to unruly children) [Lanclos 1991].

This expression recalls a time when most homes in South Louisiana were built on piers, or blocks, and when a lot of movement by boisterous children could cause the house literally to shake.

Variant: **laissez les bloques en bas de la maison!** *(leave the blocks under the house!)* [TBB].

on est parent de la fesse gauche *(we are related on the left buttock side)*
We are related, but I prefer not to claim this person as a relative.

This expression is often used in jest to refer to a relative, and is not necessarily a real rejection of the person in question.

la pêche de la bande *(the peach of the group)*
(1) The prettiest daughter of the family.
(2) The prettiest girl of a group.

un petit rien tout neuf *(a brand new little nothing)*
A nonsensical response used to avoid answering questions.

This gentler version of "none of your business" was often addressed to curious children. (I remember my own parents' response, "To see a man about a horse," when we wanted to know where they were going.) The **petit rien tout neuf** *is typically described in further detail as being:* **dans une boîte vide** *(in an empty box)*
dans une boîte ronde sans fond *(in a round, bottomless box)*
dans une petite boîte qu'a pas de fond *(in a little box which has no bottom),* *or any combination of the above.*

un petit tonnerre *(a little thunder)*
A highly active child.

See also **un tonnerre à la voile.**

petit gâteau *(little cake/cookie)*
Favorite child [Simon 1991].

portée (n.f.) *(litter)*
A large number of siblings.

This expression usually has a slightly derogatory or humorous connotation, as in **Garde voir Wilda et sa portée après sortir de la boutique!** *(Look at Wilda and her litter of kids coming out of the store!)*.

sisi (m.) à dents *(a toothed saw)*
(1) Expression used to avoid answering a question or naming something one does not wish to reveal [Reinecke 1971, Granier 1939].
(2) "A mythical trap or snare against which children were warned" [Dugas 1935].

Essentially, it is another gentle way of telling childen, "mind your own business." Although I was unable to verify its present-day use in Acadiana, it is interesting to note that Reinecke's variant **sisi à dents dans une boîte sans fond** *(a toothed saw in a bottomless box)* recalls the **petit rien tout neuf** (see above), also used in the same contexts.

un tonnerre à la voile *(a thunderbolt in the sail)*
An noisy, unruly person, typically a child.

traînasse (n.f.) *(that which drags behind)*
"A following of children, charges or dependents" [Jeansonne 1938, Granier 1939].

La nature

Nature

The nature vocabulary which Louisiana's early French-speaking settlers brought with them described a reality vastly different from that which they would encounter in their new home. This chapter shows some of the adaptations and innovations they devised to describe the land, weather, plants and animals of the area.

Chapitre 22

About weather:

balai du ciel *(broom of the sky)*
A northwest wind [Buchanan 1931]; "A northwest wind following weather disturbance and announcing return of calm" [Voohries 1949].

les boulangeries se sont battues *(the bakeries had a fight)*
There is a frost on the ground.

cassée (n.f.) du temps *(the breaking of the weather)*
The clearing up of weather [Guilbeau 1950].

chandelle de glace *(ice candle)*
Icicle.

mouiller [comme] des petits nègres [en or] *(to rain/fall [like] little [golden] Negroes)*
To rain heavily.
Variant: **tomber des petits nègres la tête en bas** *(to fall little Negroes headfirst)* [Voohries 1949].

mouiller comme si le Bon Dieu est content *(to rain as if the good Lord is happy)*
To rain heavily.
Variant: **mouiller comme si tout est content** *(to rain as if everything is happy).*

mouiller des chiens et des chats *(to rain dogs and cats)*
To rain a strong rain.

mouiller jusqu'à les chiens buvaient debout *(to rain until dogs drank standing up)*
To rain very much [PNA].
Note that the final "t" sound of **debout** is often pronounced in LF.

mouiller jusqu'à les vaches beuglent *(to rain to the point where the cows moo)*
To rain a lot [PNA].

mouiller par bailles *(to rain by tubsfull)*
To rain heavily [HD].

mouiller par baquets *(to rain buckets)*
To rain heavily [HD].
Variant: **mouiller des sieaux** *(to rain buckets)*

mouiller par barils *(to rain barrels full)*
To rain heavily [HD].

les pierres sont après brûler *(the rocks are burning)*
There is a mist or vapor rising from the ground.
This phenomenon appears particularly striking on a hot day after a rain.

le pot de chambre à Virgil *(Virgil's chamber pot)*
A place where it rains frequently [Lanclos 1992].

pris (adj.) **(taken hold)**
Describing a weather condition that will last quite a while [Parr 1940].

recevoir une saucée *(to receive a saucing)*
To get a heavy rain [Daigle 1934].

se refaire *(to make oneself again)*
To get better (of weather) [Parr 1940].
The expression is also used to speak of people recovering from illness or personal tragedy.

temps boucané *(smoky weather)*
"Gloomy, overcast weather" [Parr 1940]; "hazy weather" [Voohries 1949].

trou de la souris *(the mouse's hole)*
"East, speaking of direction from which wind comes" [Hickman 1940].

vent un à décorner un boeuf *(a wind to de-horn a bull)*
A very strong wind [Reinecke 1971].

vent de Lantier *(Lantier's wind)*
A cold northeast wind [HD].
Variant: **le vent qu'a gelé les Lantier** *(the wind that froze the Lantiers)* [HD].

vent du large *(wind from the open sea)*
Southwest wind [Hickman 1940].

vents de Carême *(Lenten winds)*
Spring winds; "March winds."
Since having learned this expression from my friend RJG, I've been amazed at how often the arrival of Spring winds in Louisiana has coincided more frequently with the arrival of Lent than with the month of March.

Flora and fauna:

bébette (n.f.)
Animal or insect (in child's vocabulary) [Guilbeau 1950].

bétaille
(1) Insect [Granier 1939].
(2) Animal or creature.

chouce de miel *(a honey stump)*
Bee hive [Hickman 1940].
Chouce is the LF version of the IF **souche**. It can also be spelled **chousse**.

les fils de la Vierge *(Virgin's thread)*
Threads of white filament which are sometimes seen floating in the air in the spring.
They are actually threads of silk produced by certain species of moths after their eggs hatch. The newly hatched larva spin the silk and remain attached to it as it is carried by the wind, allowing for an efficient dispersal of their population.

jarretière de la Sainte Vierge *(the Holy Virgin's garter belt)*
Ribbon grass or sweetheart grass [Bernard 1933].

maison de crapaud *(toad house)*
Mushroom; toadstool [Jeansonne 1938].

pousser en parcage *(to push into pen)*
To take a cow to the bull for mating [Granier 1939].

tasso *(dried meat)*
Any skinny animal [Hurst 1938].
Tasso is a culinary specialty of Louisiana's southwest prairies, made famous by the recipes of Chef Paul Prudhomme. Though the term originally designated a type of dried pork or beef, today's tasso is usually smoked. Considered a delicacy by many, nevertheless, its twisted,wrinkled appearance would not be considered attractive.

tcho-tcho
Suckling pig [Jeansonne 1938].

une corde échappée *(a dropped cord)*
(1) An animal that has been deliberately lost and is wandering the streets.
(2) An unintelligent person [Lanclos 1992].

L'abondance et l'excès

Abundance and Excess

*Cajuns and Creoles are known for working hard and playing hard, and their language
has an abundance of ways of describing such exuberance.*

à [la] bride abbatue *(with the bridle loose)*
Very rapidly and carelessly.
This expression dates back to at least 17th century France.
Variant: **à la bride molle** [PNA].

à tire larigot
In great quantity; a lot.
The expression is well-known in IF and dates back to at least the 16th century, where it first referred to drinking alcohol in great quantity, but later evolved to the more general sense of "abundance" understood in LF.

arrêtez votre tactac! *(stop your popcorn!)*
Stop all the talking!
Usually said to a group. **Tactac** can refer to any kind of noisy chatter.

avoir des tripes dans les pieds *(to have intestines in one's feet)*
To be a big eater [Faulk 1977].

avoir la langue trop longue *(to have a too long tongue)*
To talk too much [Daigle 1934].

avoir le diable dans le corps *(to have the devil in one's body)*
To be mischeivous, hyperactive (particularly of a child).
It can also mean "to be of an evil nature", though this appears to be less frequent and more literal. According to Duneton 1990, the association of this expression with extreme agitation and activity can be documented as early as the 14th century, related to the supposed agitation of a body diabolically possessed. In the Acadian region of Prince Edward Island in maritime Canada, **le diable dans le corps** is a celebration featuring music and dance, conducted as part of their annual **Festival Acadien**.

avoir le pouce dans la bouche, l'autre dans le derrière *(to have one thumb in the mouth, the other in the behind)*
To have too many things to do and not enough time to do them [Soileau 1975].

avoir un bon coup de fourchette *(to have a good fork technique)*
To be a big eater, a glutton [Brandon 1955].

bal et bazar et course et bataille *(dance and bazaar and race and fight)*
A lot of different activities [MXB].

brûler la chandelle aux deux bouts *(to burn the candle at both ends)*
(1) To throw away one's fortune.
(2) To do too much activity; to overdo fun and/or work.
Variants: **brûler la chandelle dessus les deux bouts** *(to burn the candle on both ends)*
brûler le bâton des deux bouts *(to burn the candle at both ends)*
brûler le bâton de deux bouts *(to burn the stickon both ends)*
[Brandon 1955].

c'est comme les cheveux sur la tête *(it's like the hairs on your head)*
There are some in abundance.

cancan (n.m.)
Fiasco; a rowdy event.

carabiné (adj.)
(1) Excellent and abundant, usually said of a meal [Granier 1939].
(2) Extravagant; excessive [Jeansonne 1938].

carnage (n.m.) *(carnage)*
Hubbub; disturbance; noise (made by children) [Babin 1937].

comme des carencros autour d'une charogne *(like vultures around a carcass)*
Describes a large number, usually of people ready to take advantage of a bad situation [HD].
Variant: **comme des carencros derrière une charogne** *(like vultures behind a carcass)*.

cul passe sus la tête *(ass passes over the head)*
Always "on the go"; very energetic.
Semantically, this one seems linked to the 16th century **aller de cul et de tête**, which is no longer in current usage in France [Rey and Chantreau 1979], but which conveys the same meaning. Variant: **cul par-dessus la tête** *(ass over head)*.

défonceur de portes ouvertes *(one who breaks down open doors)*
(1) A rough, brutish person; one who uses excess force.
(2) One who makes a big show of doing something which is not really difficult; a braggart.
Variants: **défonceur d'une porte ouverte** *(one who breaks down an open door)*
défonceur de portes rouvertes *(one who breaks down open doors)*
casseur de barrières ouvertes *(one who breaks down open fences)*.

en avoir par dessus la tête *(to have some over the head)*
(1) To have a large quantity of something [Saucier 1956].
(2) To have too much (to do) [PNA].

écraser la mûre *(to crush the blackberry)*
(1) To have an abundance of something, such as money.
(2) To have a lot of choice in a situation.
I was very puzzled as to the possible origins of this phrase until the spring of 1994, a particularly good blackberry season. "I can't believe all the berries," I remarked to a friend while out picking, "I'm stepping on as many as I'm picking!" Sure enough, **j'écrasais la mûre**. In Quebec, **"J'ai écrasé la mûre et bu le jus toute la journée! (I crushed the berry and drank the juice all day.)** [MD], means "I haven't done a thing all day!"

en patate *(in potatoes)*
In excess; in great quantity.
Examples: **soûl en patate** ("very drunk"), **fou en patate** ("very crazy").

étouffeur de canards morts *(a strangler of dead ducks)*
Someone who overdoes things, exaggerates his actions.
This syntactical structure is repeated in a number of derogatory expressions to describe people. See also **chiqueur de lavettes grasses** and **défonceur de portes ouvertes**.

être à rang d'oignons *(to be in rows of onions)*
To be assembled in a large crowd [Parr 1940].

faire des fions
(1) To take unnecessary pains; to make unnecessary efforts [Calais 1968].
(2) To put on airs.
Variant: **prendre des fions.**

faire des fleurs *(to make flowers)*
To make something seem better than it is by exaggeration.

faire des hélas *(to make "alas")*
To exclaim over something or someone, usually in praise.

faire l'artillerie *(to do the artillery)*
To make a lot of noise [Brandon 1955].

faire les quatre cent coups *(to do the four hundred blows)*
(1) To do all sorts of things.
(2) To act mischievously, to make a lot of noise.
Usually said of children's misbehavior.

faire rougarou *(to play the werewolf)*
To carouse, to go chasing about at night.
The unsavory character of werewolves underlies yet another expression, **en rougarou** *(in werewolf)* , which means "in heat, in rut" [Granier 1939]. In France, the expression **courir le garou** evoked the same idea [Duschesne and LeGuay 1989]. Note that **rougarou** is from the IF **loupgarou**. The "l" and "r" sounds in LF are formed in similar positions in the mouth, and this same assimilation occurs with other LF words such as **rabourer (labourer IF)** and **carculer (calculer IF)**.

faire toute une histoire {de quelque chose} *(to make a whole story {of something})*
To exaggerate or overreact [Reinecke 1971].

gagner le sucre *(to win the sugar/candy)*
To show oneself as outstanding or superior; "to win the prize" [BGM].
This would be used, for example in complimenting someone on a job well done: **"Là, t'as gagné le sucre"** *(You win the prize).*

gros yeux *(big eyes)*
Greedy, gluttonous.

manger à ventre déboutonné *(to eat with the belly unbuttoned)*
Saucier 1956 includes this expression in her collection without explanation, but it must surely refer to eating heartily, if not greedily.

manger à pleine gueule *(to eat full-faced)*
To eat greedily [ED].
In LF, the first consonant sound in **gueule** is usually pronounced like the "j" sound in "judge."

manger comme quatre *(to eat like four)*
To have a large appetite [Saucier 1956, Reinecke 1971].

manger comme un cochon *(to eat like a pig)*
To eat a lot [PF].

manger comme un ours
To eat a lot [PNA].

mettre les petits plats dans les gros *(to put the little dishes in the big)*
(1) To cook a lot of food, usually because there will be company.
(2) To cook an amount of food then to stretch it for unexpected company [Lanclos 1992].
In IF, **mettre les petits plats dans les grands**, which Reinecke 1971 has also documented in the New Orleans area elliptically as **mettre les petits dans les grands,** means "to go to great lengths to feed or entertain someone." In such elaborate banquet meals, several plates are nested at a table setting, each one to be removed as the next course is served. In rural Acadiana, people of more modest means kept the expression, but adapted it to their own casual style of impromptu hospitality.

midi à quatorze heures *(noon at two p.m.)*
Tiresome chattering [JJG].
See also **chanter des midi à quatorze heures.**

par charretée *(by the wagon full)*
Plenty [Viator 1935].

pèse bouton, paie couillon! *(push button, pay fool!)*
Fancy gadgets are not worth the money one pays for them.
This expression seems to have gotten its start with the introduction of cars with electric windows and controls.

péter à cul cassé *(to fart until one's ass breaks)*
To brag; to exaggerate [RL].

péter plus haut que son nez *(to fart higher than one's nose)*
(1) To try to do things that are beyond one's social or financial means.
(2) To try to "keep up with the Joneses."

s'en foutre une bosse
To do something in excess, such as eating.

tambouille (n.f.)
A potful; plenty [Granier 1939].
Variant spelling: **tombouille.** In IF, **tambouille** describes mediocre cooking, though it's not hard to make the connection between these two meanings, since good cooks know that it is difficult to maintain the quality of a dish when it is cooked in large quantity.

tout décarabiné
With all one's might; unrestrainedly [Guilbeau 1950].

Lagnappe

Lagniappe

*From the Spanish **la ñapa**, **lagnappe** is something extra, the baker's dozen, a little surprise thrown in for good measure. Included here are expressions which didn't fit into any of the chapter themes, and some which seem to be in a category of their own.*

avoir tous leur tête dans le même bonnet *(to have all their heads in the same bonnet)*
(Of several people) to think alike; to be in complete agreement.

ça aurait pas pris un Yinqui *(that wouldn't have taken a Yankee)*
That's easy to do; that's easy to understand [HR].

ça coupe aussi bien que mon doigt *(that cuts as well as my finger)*
It doesn't cut; it is not very sharp.

ça coupe comme la jambe à ma grand-mère *(that cuts like my grandmother's leg)*
It doesn't cut; it is not very sharp.
The very similar structure **couper comme un genou** *(to cut like a knee)* cited in Rey and Chantreau 1979, and the expressions **couper comme le genou de magrand'** *(to cut like my granny's knee)* and **couper comme le mollet de magrand'** *(to cut like my granny's calf)* mentioned in Duneton 1990 are expressions used in France to describe figuratively something which is supposed to cut but does not.
Variant: **ça coupe comme la jambe de ma grand-mère** *(that cuts like my grandmother's leg)*

ça coupe comme la langue de ma grand-mère *(that cuts like my grandmother's tongue)*
It is very sharp (literally or figuratively) [MBG].
In a wry twist on the previous expression, the metaphorical image of a "sharp tongue" can be used to describe things that are literally sharp.

ça coupe comme une jambe de chien *(that cuts like a dog's leg)*
It doesn't cut; it is not very sharp.

ça crève les yeux *(that hurts one's eyes)*
That's obvious [Saucier 1956].

ça prend pas un avocat *(that doesn't take a lawyer)*
That's obvious; that's easy to understand.

chercher à pied et à cheval *(to search on foot and on horseback)*
To search extensively and exhaustively for something [Simon 1991].
In France, a similar 19th century construction **à pied, à cheval et en voiture** *(on foot, on horseback and by car)* is used to mean "completely and totally." According to Duneton 1990, it has its origins in the formula which inns used to advertise that they welcomed all travelers, regardless of their means of transportation.

donner de la confiture aux cochons *(to give jelly/sweets to pigs)*
To "throw pearls before swine;" to match up someone of quality with someone much less worthy or attractive.
Several informants gave the marriage of a beautiful, young woman to a much older man as an example.

faire une saucée *(to do a saucing)*
To make a short visit.
See also: **recevoir une saucée.**

une grenouille de bénitier *(a baptismal font frog)*
A woman who volunteers often at church.
Edouard 1967 gives this IF definition: "a lady of a certain age who comes to find in the house of God a peace which she has given up finding in her own home (derogatory)."

l'homme qu'a vu l'homme qu'a vu l'ours *(the man who saw the man who saw the bear)*
The unknown source of a third-hand story or piece of gossip.
Suggesting that **l'homme qu'a vu l'homme qu'a vu l'ours** *is the source of a piece of information is a humourous way of questioning its reliability. Pascal Fuselier, in one of his "Crow's Nest" editorials, mentions a similar expression,* **c'est lui l'homme qu'a vu l'ours qu'a étranglé le lion par la queue** *(he's the man who saw the bear who strangled the lion by the tail) as a light-hearted mocking of a braggart.*

il y a plus d'une manière d'étouffer un chien à part lui donner une saucisse *(There's more than one way to choke a dog than giving him a sausage.)*
There is another way to deal with the situation; "there's more than one way to skin a cat" [GP].

il y a toujours du feu dans la cheminée *(there's still fire in the fireplace)*
The person in question is still interested and active sexually.
This is usually a reference to an older person.

il y a un cabri dans le maïs *(there's a goat in the corn)*
Said when one's underpants have crawled up and become stuck between one's buttocks (a predicament known in colloquial English as "a wedgie.")

pacane *(pecan)*
Nothing.
This expression is probably derived from the first syllable of the word, which sounds like the negative particle **pas.** *As with most negatives in Cajun French, the* **pas** *frequently*

reinforces the expression, as in **J'ai pas vu pacane!** *(I didn't see a thing!)* or **Elle a pas dit pacane!** *(She didn't say anything!).*

passer par la porte [d']en arrière *(to go through the back door)*
To achieve something by non-traditional or unofficial means.
It is said for example, that one becomes a Cajun **par le sang, par le mariage, ou par la porte en arrière** *(by blood, by marriage or by the back door).*

le prêtre dit pas sa messe deux fois *(the priest does not say his Mass twice)*
Said when one refuses to repeat what he/she has already said
[Simon 1991].

un rêve de poulet *(a chicken's dream)*
An unrealistic idea or plan.

la roue tourne *(the wheel turns)*
Things change [Saucier 1956].

se coller un temps *(to stick oneself a time)*
To have a good time [Jeansonne 1938]

se ressembler comme deux gouttes d'eau *(to resemble each other like two drops of water)*
Of a pair, to resemble each other very closely.
This expression is well known in IF.

le sirop et biscuits cassent pas égal *(the syrup and the biscuits don't even out)*
Vengeance never "evens out" a wrong.
The allusion is to eating biscuits with syrup, when one always ends up with a little more syrup than biscuit (or vice versa), which necessitates serving oneself more biscuit, leading to an excess which requires more syrup, etc. The adage seems particularly appropriate as a metaphor for the futility of long-standing family feuds.

tamiser la vie *(to sift life)*
To get the most out of life; to live life to its fullest [Lanclos 1992].

tomber dans le panneau *(to fall in the trap)*
To happen advantageously [Viator 1935].
According to Duneton 1990, the term **panneau** refers to a type of small animal trap and dates back to 17th century France, where the expressions **donner dans le panneau** *(to give in the trap)* and **tomber dans le panneau** *(to fall in the trap)* both meant "to be trapped or duped by a trick."

Informants

Name	Code	Parish
Ancelet, Barry	BA	LAFAYETTE
Armand, Lester	LA	EVANGELINE, ALLEN
Aucoin, Preston	PNA	EVANGELINE
Babin, Onita Robichaux	ONI	TERREBONNE
Beaugh, Delia Trahan	DB	ACADIA
Bergeron, Pete	PB	ACADIA
Billeaudeau, Bee	BB	ACADIA
Billeaudeau, Rita Richard	BBF	ACADIA
Bourgeois, Easton "Ti-Boy"	TBB	ACADIA, LAFAYETTE
Breaux, Sue	SB	VERMILION
Broussard, J. Maxie	MXB	LAFAYETTE
Broussard, Theresa	TB	VERMILION
Brown, Bruce	BRB	EVANGELINE, ST. LANDRY
Brown, Cynthia	CB	EVANGELINE, LAFAYETTE
Brown, Merzie Billeaudeau	MBB	EVANGELINE
Brown, Ryan	RB	ST. LANDRY
Browning, AnnaBelle	ABR	TERREBONNE
Cancienne, Bernice A.	BAC	TERREBONNE
Comeaux, Earl**	EC	VERMILION
Conner, Cinderella Chiasson*	CCC	VERMILION
Cormier, Antoine*	ACO	VERMILION
Daigle, Hilda	HD	ACADIA
Daigle, Pierre V.	PVD	ACADIA
David, Marc	MD	VERMILION
Deshotels, Elby*	ED	EVANGELINE
Domingue, Winona	WD	LAFAYETTE
Douet, Kenneth	KD	ST. MARTIN, LAFAYETTE
Dugas, Paul	PD	LAFAYETTE
Dugas, Witness*	WDU	LAFAYETTE
Broussard, Earlene	EBE	VERMILION
Fuselier, Elvin Joseph "Pascal"	PF	EVANGELINE
Fontenot, Sue	FF	ST. LANDRY
Foret, Burton	BFO	EVANGELINE
Guidry, Kenneth	KAG	VERMILION
Guidry, Mildred Breaux	MBG	VERMILION
Guidry, Richard J.	RJG	VERMILION, LAFAYETTE
Guidry, Roy	JRG	VERMILION
Hulin, Ronnie	RH	LAFAYETTE
Jambon, Kirby	KJ	LAFOURCHE
LaFleur, Florence Brown	FBL	EVANGELINE
Lanclos, David	DLA	ST. LANDRY
Leblanc, Rita Romero	RRL	IBERIA, ST. MARTIN
LeBlanc, Robert	RL	EAST TEXAS, LAFOURCHE
Ledet, Laïse	LLE	TERREBONNE
Lemoine, Burnell	BL	AVOYELLES
Lormand, Lucille	LL	ST. MARTIN
Marcotte, Marion	MM	??

Menard, Louella	LM	VERMILION
Mhire, Evelyn	EM	ST. MARTIN
Mounier, Brenda Gayle	BGM	EVANGELINE, LAFAYETTE
Nagata, Jenora Brown	JBN	EVANGELINE, ST. LANDRY
Olivier, Louise	LO	??
Patin, Fleurette	FP	ST. MARTIN
Phillip Hosea*	HP	EVANGELINE
Pitre, Glen	GP	LAFOURCHE
Pitre, Irvin	IP	TERREBONNE
Pontier, Bil	BP	AVOYELLES
Préjean, Janice	JP	LAFAYETTE
Putnam, Helena	HEP	EVANGELINE
Reed, Hube*	HR	EVANGELINE
Reed, Irving *	IR	EVANGELINE
Reed, Revon*	RR	EVANGELINE
Saltzman, Alphonsine	AB	VERMILION
Savoy, Shirley	SS	LAFAYETTE
Sebastien, Roy	RS	ST. LANDRY
Simon, Allen	AS	VERMILION, LAFAYETTE
Sr. Citizens' Group	TBN	TERREBONNE
Tally, Bill	BT	ST. MARTIN
Terrebonne, Oralie Cheramie	OCT	LAFOURCHE
Toups, Octave	OT	LAFOURCHE
Trahan, Lucie M	LMT	ASSUMPTION
Trahan, M.C. **	MCT	VERMILION
Trotter, Phoebe Beaugh	PBT	ACADIA, LAFAYETTE
Valincour, Milton	MV	ACADIA, JEFFERSON DAVIS
Valincour, Odile	OV	ACADIA, JEFFERSON DAVIS
Viator, Etienne	EV	ST. LANDRY
Vincent, Clyde	CV	EAST TEXAS
Wiltz, Louisiana	LW	ST. MARTIN
Young, Edna	EY	EVANGELINE

Names marked by asterisks denote informants interviewed by researchers other than the author. Information is taken from records of interviews housed in the archives of the Center for Acadian and Creole Folklore, University of Southwestern Louisiana.

*Ancelet Collection (1974-   )
**Tang Collection (1984)

Louisiana Collections Cited

Babin, Lawrence. 1937. *A glossary of the French spoken on Grand Isle.* MA thesis, Louisiana State University.

Bernard, Lorene Marie. 1933. *A study of Louisiana French in Lafayette Parish.* MA thesis, Louisiana State University.

Brandon, Elizabeth. 1955. *Moeurs et langue de la Paroisse Vermillion en Louisiane.* PhD dissertation, Université Laval.

Buchanan, Ann Spotswood. 1931. *Lafayette Parish: some things that belong to the early days of Lafayette Parish.* MA thesis, Louisiana State University.

Calais, Gayle Dolores. 1968. *The Acadian French of the Parks, Louisiana area.* MA thesis, University of Southwestern Louisiana.

Coco, Eunice R. 1933. *An etymological glossary of the variants from standard French used in Avoyelles Parish.* MA thesis, Louisiana State University.

Daigle, Anna T. 1934. *Folklore and etymological glossary of the variants from standard French in Jefferson Davis Parish.* MA thesis, Louisiana State University.

Daigle, Jules. 1992 *Cajun self-taught.* Ville Platte: Soileau Publications, Inc.

Deblanc, Bertrand F. 1935. *A glossary of variants from standard French found in St. Martin Parish, Louisiana.* MA thesis, Louisiana State University.

Dugas, Alice M. 1935. *A glossary of the variants from standard French used in the parish of St. James.* MA thesis, Louisiana State University.

Faulk, James D. 1977. *Cajun French I.* Abbeville: Cajun Press, Inc.

Granier, Ervin Louis. 1939. *A glossary of the French spoken in St. John Parish.* MA thesis, Louisiana State University.

Guilbeau, John J. 1936. *A glossary of variants from standard French in Lafourche Parish.* MA thesis, Louisiana State University.

Guilbeau, John J. 1950. *The French spoken in Lafourche Parish, Louisiana.* PhD dissertation, University of North Carolina, Chapel Hill.

Hickman, Frances H. 1940. *The French speech of Jefferson Parish.* MA thesis, Louisiana State University.

Hurst, Harry M. 1938. *A glossary of the French spoken in St. Charles Parish.* MA thesis, Louisiana State University.

Iseringhausen, Ferdinand J. 1956. *A glossary of the French spoken in Church Point, Acadia Parish, Louisiana.* MA thesis, Louisiana State University.

Jeansonne, Samuel L. 1938. *A glossary of words that vary from standard French in Avoyelles Parish* . MA thesis, Louisiana State University.

Lanclos, David. 1992 *La pacanière collection*, an unpublished collection of figurative expressions from the St. Landry area.

Loupe, Sylvain R. 1932. *Living Acadian folklore of La Côte Française* . MA thesis, Louisiana State University.

Olivier, Louise. 1937. *A glossary of variants from standard French in Saint Landry Parish* . MA thesis, Louisiana State University.

Parr, Una M. 1940. *A glossary of the variants from standard French in Terrebonne Parish: with an appendix of popular beliefs, superstitions, medicine and cooking recipes.* MA thesis, Louisiana State University.

Phillips, Hosea. 1936. *Etude du parler de la paroisse Evangeline, Louisiana.* Paris: Librairie L. Droz.

Pirkle, Marie N. 1935. *Variants from standard French common to the dialects of Lafayette Parish and Canada.* MA thesis, Louisiana State University.

Reinecke, George F. 1971. Proverbial locutions of New Orleans.French. *Louisiana Folklore Miscellany*, Vol. 3, no. 2, pp. 34-38.

Saucier, Corinne. L. 1956. *Traditions de la paroisse des Avoyelles en Louisiane.* Philadelphia: American Folklore Society.

Simon, Allen. 1991. *Nonc Allin, les dit-ons du vieux temps.* Audiocassette produced for broadcast on KRVS Radio, Lafayette, Louisiana.

Soileau, Jeanne. 1975. Proverbs and proverbial locutions of the St. Martin area. *Louisiana Folklore Miscellany*, Vol. 3, no. 4, pp. 29-34.

Trahan, Lucie M. 1936. *Etymological glossary of the variants from standard French in Assumption Parish* . MA thesis, Louisiana State University.

Trappey, Maud Marie. 1940. *The French speech of Iberia Parish.* MA thesis, Louisiana State University.

Viator, Audrey Bernard. 1935. *A glossary of neologisms, loan-words and variants from standard French in the parish of St. John the Baptist.* MA thesis, Louisiana State University.

Voohries, Edward T. 1949. *A glossary of variants from standard French in St. Martin Parish , Louisiana, followed by some of the folklore of the parish.* MA thesis, Louisiana State University.

Bibliography of Other Sources

Bergeron, Léandre. 1981. *Dictionnaire de la langue québécoise, Supplément 1981.* Montréal: VLB Editeur.

Boudreau, Ephrem. 1988. *Glossaire du vieux parler acadien.* Montréal: Editions du Fleuve.

Cellard, Jacques. 1982. *Ça mange pas de pain!* Paris: Hachette.

Daigle, Jules. 1984. *A dictionary of the Cajun language.* Ann Arbor: Edwards Brothers, Inc.

Deak, Etienne and Simone. 1959. *A dictionary of colorful French slanguage and colloquialisms.* Paris: Robert Laffont.

DesRuisseaux, Pierre. 1979. *Le livre des expressions québécoises.* Montreal: Editions Hurtubise HMH, Limitée.

Ditchy, Jay. 1932. *Les Acadiens louisianais et leur parler.* Baltimore: Institut français de Washington.

Duchesne, Alain and Thierry Leguay. 1989. *L'obsolète: dictionnaire des mots perdus.* Paris: Larousse.

Duneton, Claude. *1985. La puce à l'oreille: anthologie des expressions populaires avec leur origine* (new edition). Editions Balland.

Duneton, Claude and Sylvie Claval. 1990. *Le bouquet des expressions imagées: encyclopédie thématique des locutions figurées de la langue française.* Editions du Seuil.

Dutrieu, Jacques. 1959. *Quelle est l'origine de...?.* Paris: Editions Wesmael-Charlier.

Edouard, Robert. 1967. *Dictionnaire des injures, précédé d'un petit traité d'injurologie.* Paris: Tchou.

Hendrickson, Robert. 1987. *The facts on file encyclopedia of word and phrase origins.* New York: Facts on File Publications.

McDermott, John F. 1941. *A glossary of Mississippi Valley French 1673-1850.* St. Louis: Washington University Studies.

Read, William A. 1931. *Louisiana-French.* Baton Rouge: Louisiana State University Press.

Rey, Alain and Sophie Chantreau. 1979. *Dictionnaire des expressions et locutions.* Paris: Le Robert.

Rézeau, Pierre. 1984. *Dictionnaire des régionalismes de l'ouest entre Loire et Gironde.* Les Sables d'Olonne: Le Cercle d'Or.

Robinson, Sinclair and D. Smith. 1984. *Practical handbook of Quebec and Acadian French.* Toronto: House of Anansi Press Limited.

Rousseau, Jacques. 1971. *Le Parler canadien et le français universel.* Trois-Rivières: Editions du Bien Public.

La Société du Parler Français au Canada. 1968. *Glossaire du parler français au Canada.* Québec: Les Presses de L'Université Laval.

Index of Key Words

baratte
lâcher la baratte, 117

barbe
tu crois [que] t'as de la barbe et des crochets, 30

baril
croche comme un baril de serpents, 100
mouiller par barils, 136
vider la mer avec un baril défoncé, 117

baroque, 74

barouche
faire barouche, 10

barré
candi barré, 81
yeux barrés, 110

barrière
maigre comme un poteau de barrière, 125

bas
avoir la fale basse, 55

basset
faire le filou comme un chien basset, 101

bastringue
passer {quelqu'un} à la bastringue, 16

bataille
bal et bazar et course et bataille, 140
jeu de chien tourne en bataille, 133
vin à vingt batailles au gallon, 23

bâtard
suer comme un bâtard à une réunion de famille, 47

bateau
manquer le bateau avec le tiquette dans la main, 46

bâton
mettre des bâtons dans la roue, 64
bâton de vieillesse, 132
bûche ça à coups de bâton, 28
ça vaut pas tuer à coups de bâton, 107
casser le petit bâton, 104
fou comme un bâton, 25

battant
avoir de l'argent tambour battant, 40
faire {quelque chose} à tambour battant, 116

battre
battre la berloque, 24
battre sa gueule, 65
les boulangeries se sont battues, 136

baver
fou à baver sus sa chemise, 25

bazar
bal et bazar et course et bataille, 140

beau
faire une belle grâce, 64
faire [sa] belle, 132
il y a bel âge, 37
un [beau] coco, 81

bébé
brailler comme un petit bébé, 70
fin comme la peau d'un bébé, 124

bébette, 137

bec
avoir un nez comme un bec, 56
avoir un nez comme un bec à lancette, 56
s'en passer au bout du bec, 47

bécassine
bécassine créole, 50

bénédiction
s'il croit avoir fait l'oeuvre du Bon Dieu, qu'il espère sa bénédiction, 97

c'est pas toi qu'as fait la petite almanaque
bleue, 32
palais bleu, 108
passer du bleu de ciel avec, 46
passer une bleue, 102
sacré bleu, 30
voir [du] bleu, 48

bloque
laissez un bloque en bas de la maison, 133

boeuf
cacher son argent dans des cornes à boeuf,
40
fort comme un boeuf, 124
vent (un) à décorner un boeuf, 137

bogui
mettre le bogui avant le cheval, 65

boire
boire comme si on n'avait pas de fond, 20
boire comme un chien, 20
boire comme un poisson, 20
boire comme un tablier, 20
boire comme un trou, 20
mouiller jusqu'à les chiens buvaient debout,
136

bois
avoir l'oeil au bois, 56

boisson
en boisson, 21
sac à boisson

bol
cogner {quelqu'un} comme une bol de
merde, 93
mettre son nez dans le bol, 64

bombe. See bomme

bomme
bomme à café, 50
bomme queue raide, 50

bon
avoir bonne idée, 74
avoir un bon coup de fourchette, 140
bon comme (de) l'or, 121
bon comme la vie, 121
bon comme son père, 121
bon comme un ange, 121
Bon Dieu seigneur, 28
bon[ne] à marier, 132
le Bon Dieu descend pas pour bûcher, 14
mouiller comme si le Bon Dieu est content,
136
pas assez bon pour faire du savon, 107
pas avoir une bonne idée, 26
s'il croit avoir fait l'oeuvre du Bon Dieu, qu'il
espère sa bénédiction, 97
tirer la bonne aventure, 84

bonbon
cul [de] bonbon, 81

bonnet
avoir tous leur tête dans le même bonnet,
146

boscot, 57

bossal
prendre un bossal, 51

bosse
s'en foutre une bosse, 144

botte
avoir du foin dans ses bottes, 40
cailler la botte, 112
paner la botte, 113
tomber en botte, 113

boucane
mettre de la boucane en sac, 69

boucané
temps boucané, 137

éclair
passer comme un éclair, 102
tonnerre et z'éclairs, 30

école
maîtresse d'école

écorce
mets pas ton doigt entre l'arbre et l'écorce, 11

écraser
écraser la mûre, 142
tonnerre m'écrase, 30
tu vas jamais écraser les chaises dans le sénat, 31

écrevisse
rouge comme une écrevisse, 127

effleuré
avoir les narines effleurées, 91

égal
le sirop et biscuits cassent pas égal, 148

égaré
avoir les yeux égarés, 56

église
pauvre comme un rat [d'église], 41

éléphant
avoir des oreilles d'éléphant, 54
fort comme un éléphant, 124

embêter, *82*

embeurrer, *101*

emplâtre, *76*
emplâtre comme du goudron, 123

enfance
en enfance, 25

enfant
enfant du deuxième lit, 132
enfant inconnu, 82

enfilé. See **afilé**

enragé
fâché comme un chien enragé, 94
faire manger de la vache enragée, 95
faire manger du chien enragé, 95

ensemble
faire chaudière ensemble, 10

enterrement
mieux que ça serait un enterrement, 3

enterrer
c'est là où mon nombril est enterré, 132

entêté
entêté comme un mulet, 123

envaler. See also **avaler**
rire comme un mulet qu'a envalé des ronces, 127

épaule
changer son fusil d'épaule, 93
mettre l'épaule à la roue, 64

épingle
être sur les épingles, 94
on peut pas y mettre une épingle, 38

équilibre
perdre l'équilibre, 26

espoir
vivre en espoir et mourir comme un vieux chien, 48

esprit
ça c'est assez bête, si ça tombe à quatre pattes ça va pas avoir assez d'esprit pour se lever, 75

lait
blanc comme du lait, 120
jambe de lait, 59
un buveur de lait, 21

lampe
*avoir des jambes comme des globes de
lampe, 54*
on a plein d'huile dans la lampe, 5

lancette
avoir un nez comme un bec à lancette, 56

langue
avaler la langue, 90
avoir la langue comme une vipère, 108
avoir la langue trop longue, 140
langue de serpent, 108
pas avoir la langue d'amarrée, 65

Lantier
vent de Lantier, 137

lapin
ça vaut pas le lapin du curé, 106

lard
faire du lard, 58

large
au large, 37
large comme deux doigts, 38
large comme mes deux fesses, 38
vent du large, 137

larigot
à tire larigot, 140

larme
avoir larme près de l'oeil, 104
brailler à chaudes larmes, 70
brasser mer et larmes, 44

lavette
chiqueur de lavettes grasses, 76

lavure, *50*
aimer comme cochon aime lavure, 120

léger
léger comme une plume, 125
léger comme une poussière, 125

lever
c'est l'heure qu'on lève la paille, 5
c'est l'heure qu'on lève la patte, 5
*ça c'est assez bête, si ça tombe à quatre
pattes ça va pas avoir assez d'esprit pour se
lever, 75*
lever la queue, 67
lever le pied, 67
se lever sur le mauvais pied, 96

licher, *101*

lilas
attraper un coup de lilas, 104

linge
blanc comme un linge, 121
chiquer du vieux linge, 104

lire
lire un catéchisme, 16

lis
la fleur de lis, 132

lit
enfant du deuxième lit, 132

long
avoir la langue trop longue, 140
avoir le nez long, 74
avoir un pet en long, 92

loupgarou. See rougarou

lourd
avoir un coeur lourd, 91

manger les grillots avec le tactac, 87
se manger de rage, 96

manier
manier la tapette, 22

manière
il y a plus d'une manière d'étouffer un chien
à part lui donner une saucisse, 147

manivelle
monter sa manivelle, 65

manne
sérieux comme une manne de tripes, 127

manquer
manquer le bateau avec le tiquette dans la
main, 46

marais
dételer le wagon au milieu du marais, 116

marcher
il faut qu'elle marche deux fois à la même
place pour faire un ombrage, 59

mari
prends mari, prends pays, 11

Marie
Sainte Vierge Marie, 30

marier
bon[ne] à marier, 132

maringouin
si c'est pas les maringouins, c'est les
chouboulures, 47

marron
partir marron, 67

massacrer
massacrer la couenne, 16

matin
un de ces quatre matins, 37

matinée
faire la grasse matinée, 62

maudit

Maurin
Taupin vaut Maurin, 108

mauvais
faire du mauvais sang, 94
mauvaise comme la gale, 126
mauvaise comme un(e) serpent à sonnette,
126
mauvaise comme une guêpe, 126
mauvaise comme une puce, 126
se lever sur le mauvais pied, 96

melasse
doucement comme la melasse dans janvier,
122

membré
membré comme une tortue de rosée, 59

même
avoir tous leur tête dans le même bonnet
ême, 146
ça chie dans le même sac, 8

memère
si on peut pas téter maman, il faut téter
memère, 47

menteur
menteur comme un dentiste, 100

mentir
mentir comme un dentiste, 101

mer
brasser mer et larmes, 44
brasser mer et par terre, 44
c'est pas toi qu'as salé la mer, 32
vider la mer avec un baril défoncé, 117

merci
merci, Bon Dieu

mors
partir mors aux dents, 67

mort
ça vaut pas les quatre fers d'un cheval mort,
106
coeur, 91
étouffeur de canards morts, 142
être venu un fil de sa mort, 45
fort comme la mort, 124
la mort n'a pas de faim/fin, 11
le docteur après la mort, 4
poser sa chique [et faire le mort], 66
se placer, 11
son vanteur est mort, 97
traître comme la mort, 102

mortel
vilain comme les sept péchés mortels, 128

mot
avoir des mots, 14

mou
dormir comme une caille molle, 62

mouiller
mouiller comme si le Bon Dieu est content,
136
mouiller des chiens et des chats, 136
mouiller jusqu'à les chiens buvaient debout,
136
mouiller jusqu'à les vaches beuglent, 136
mouiller par bailles, 136
mouiller par baquets, 136
mouiller par barils, 136
mouiller [comme] des petits nègres, 136

mouliner
mouliner la queue du chien, 69

mourir
vivre en espoir et mourir comme un vieux
chien, 48

mouroir
être sus le mouroir, 45

mulâtre
estomac de mulâtre, 50

mulet
dételer le mulet dans le milieu des rangs,
116
entêté comme un mulet, 123
faire son mulet, 70
fort comme un mulet, 124
quand on a pas de cheval on monte mulet,
87
rire comme un mulet qu'a envalé des ronces,
127

mûre
écraser la mûre, 142

musique
comme un papier de musique, 122

N
nanane, *50*

narine
avoir les narines effleurées, 91
avoir les narines ouvertes, 91
se souffler dans les narines, 18

nègre
mouiller [comme] des petits nègres, 136
orteil de nègre, 50
suer comme un nègre à la messe

neige
blanc comme la neige, 121

nenaine
être la nenaine, 45
ta nenaine est caille, 30

nerf
fait du nerf et de la babiche, 87

neuf
travailler comme (un) neuf, 128
un petit rien tout neuf, 133

orteil
orteil de nègre, 50

ouragan
il y a un ouragan dans la Chine, 38
un pet dans un ouragan, 105

ours
l'homme qu'a vu l'homme qu'a vu l'ours, 147
manger comme un ours, 143

ouvert
avoir des oreilles comme un taxi avec les
deux portes ouvertes, 54
avoir les narines ouvertes, 91
défonceur de portes ouvertes, 141

P
pacane, 147

paillasse
mettre le feu à la paillasse, 68

paille
à la paille, 62
c'est l'heure qu'on lève la paille, 5
casser la paille, 8
mettre le feu à la paille, 68

pain
gagner son pain par la sueur de son front, 41
un pain de sucre, 102

palais
palais bleu, 108

palonnier
chier sur le palonnier, 116

paner
paner la botte, 113

panier
sot comme un panier percé, 77

panneau
être dans le panneau, 77
tomber dans le panneau, 148

paon
amoureux comme un paon, 120
faquin comme un paon, 123
fier comme un paon, 123

papier
comme un papier de musique, 122

papillote
faire de papillotes, 70
mettre sa bouche en papillotes, 96

Pâques
faire Pâques avant Carême, 83

parc
avoir pas plus de chance qu'une sauterelle
dans un parc de dindes, 44

parcage
pousser en parcage, 138

parent
on est parent de la fesse gauche, 133

Paris
être dans le Paris des oies, 62
le postier à Paris va jamais voir ça, 105

parler
en parlant des anges, on voit leurs ailes, 4
en parlant du diable, on voit sa queue, 4
parler comme du tactac, 65
quand on parle de la bête, on voit sa tête, 4

paroisse
dans les quatre paroisses, 38

partance
donner une partance, 64

partir
partir avant les guêpes, 67

sacrer une gratte, 17

saint
c'est comme Saint Roch et son chien, 8
dégréer Saint Pierre pour gréer Saint Paul, 86
faire le cochon de Saint Antoine, 66
il doit à Dieu et ses saints, 41
jarretière de la Sainte Vierge, 138
que la Sainte Vierge doit honnir, 29
Sainte Vierge Marie, 30
une sainte mitouche, 97

salade, 17

sang
faire du mauvais sang, **94**

sangsue
collé comme un sangsue, 122

sauce
être dans sa sauce, 93

saucé
faire une saucée, 147
recevoir une saucée, 137
saucé, 22

saucisse
amarrer ses chiens avec des saucisses, 40
il y a plus d'une manière d'étouffer un chien à part lui donner une saucisse, 147

sauter
sauter crapaud, 102
sauter le manche à balai, 11

sauterelle
avoir pas plus de chance qu'une sauterelle dans un parc de dindes, 44

savate
traîner les savates, 105

savon
pas assez bon pour faire du savon, 107

sec
avoir l'oeil sec, 90
la piste est sèque, 38
poisson à terre sèque, 46

seigneur
Bon Dieu seigneur, 28

sellé
c'est sellé et bridé, 112

sénat
tu vas jamais casser les chaises dans le sénat, 31

sept
vilain comme les sept péchés mortels, 128

serein
coucher au serein, 70

sérieux
sérieux comme une manne de tripes, 127

serpent
croche comme un baril de serpents, 100
être comme un(e) serpent à sonnette, 123
langue de serpent, 108
mauvaise comme un(e) serpent à sonnette, 126

sieau

siffler
siffler dans le vent, 69

singo
faire singo, 63

sirop
être dans son sirop, 93
le sirop et biscuits cassent pas égal, 148

sisi
sisi (m.) à dents, 134

Y

yeast
yeast macaque, 51

yeux
avoir froid aux yeux, 90
avoir les yeux dolents, 56
avoir les yeux égarés, 56, 91
avoir les yeux gouaires, 56
avoir les yeux noirs comme des socos, 56
ça crève les yeux, 146
flamber les yeux, 70, 95
gros yeux, 143

yeux barrés, 110

Yinqui
ça aurait pas pris un Yinqui, 146

Z

zinc
cheval habillé en zinc, 81
vache habillée en zinc, 110

zinzin
avoir les zinzins, 91

To order *Tonnerre mes chiens!*

By postal service:
Complete and mail this form, along with your check, money order or credit card authorization, to:
Renouveau Publishing
P.O. Box 617
Ville Platte, LA 70586

By FAX (credit card orders only): Complete and fax this form to: (318) 363-6812

(To inquire by e-mail about international and bulk orders, write to: **cajungloss@aol.com**)

Name _____

Address _____

City _____ State ____ Zip _____

Telephone: _____

E-mail address: _____

Number of copies: _____ X $16.95   = _____
State and local sales tax (**La. shipments only**) _____ % = _____
Shipping: $4 for first book and $1 for each additional copy _____

                                    TOTAL   = _____
Payment: —— check —— Visa —— MasterCard
Name on card: _____
Card # _____ Exp. Date ___ /___
Authorizing signature: _____